Eating Disorders - Current Controversies

Edited by Paul Robinson

Published in London, United Kingdom

Eating Disorders - Current Controversies
http://dx.doi.org/10.5772/intechopen.1000531
Edited by Paul Robinson

Contributors
Adaeze Bradshaw, Antonello Colli, Aurora Gil, Chen-Hang Yuan, Chen-Jun Liu, Daniela Gómez, Giulia Gagliardini, Hatice Toprak, Iakovina Koutoufa, Jacinta Tan, Jess Griffiths, Li Zhao, Melina Vogel, Pamela Pino, Paul Robinson, Rui-Xin Huang, Shan-Shan Mao, Şükrü Salih Toprak

First published in London, United Kingdom, 2025 by IntechOpen
IntechOpen is the global imprint of INTECHOPEN LIMITED, registered in England and Wales, registration number: 11086078, 167-169 Great Portland Street, London, W1W 5PF, United Kingdom

For EU product safety concerns: IN TECH d.o.o., Prolaz Marije Krucifikse Kozulić 3, 51000 Rijeka, Croatia, info@intechopen.com or visit our website at intechopen.com.

British Library Cataloguing-in-Publication Data
A catalogue record for this book is available from the British Library

Eating Disorders - Current Controversies
Edited by Paul Robinson
p. cm.

This title is part of the Nervous System and Mental Health Book Series, Volume 3
Series Editor: Toshikazu Shinba

Print ISBN 978-1-83634-707-1
Online ISBN 978-1-83634-706-4
eBook (PDF) ISBN 978-1-83634-708-8
ISSN 3050-2985

IntechOpen Book Series

Nervous System and Mental Health

Volume 3

Aims and Scope of the Series

Mental health is frequently linked to the nervous system. Conversely, disturbances in the nervous system often lead to mental health problems. However, this linkage is not as clear as it is commonly accepted. Mental health is usually described using subjective terms, which are based on psychological and psychiatric symptomatology. Diagnosis of a mental illness is made through the presence of the subjective symptoms characterizing the illness.

On the other hand, the nervous system has been deeply investigated using objective measures, including molecular, genetic, imaging, pharmacological and physiological ones. It is essential to combine objective views of the nervous system with subjective perspectives on mental health to develop an integrative approach to understanding human cognitive functions and achieving overall well-being. In this book series, experts in various fields of the nervous system and mental health will present their views on these challenging topics.

Meet the Series Editor

Dr. Toshikazu Shinba is a psychiatrist and neuroscientist who has been working in both clinical and basic research fields. He has been affiliated with the Tokyo Institute of Psychiatry, Department of Neurophysiology and Stress Disorders Project, and now works as a psychiatrist at Shizuoka Saiseikai General Hospital, Department of Psychiatry. The primary focus of his research is the electrophysiological analysis of attention and arousal in both humans and rodents. In clinical research, EEG, heart rate variability and skin conductance have been measured in mental disorders and arousal/consciousness disturbances. In basic research, single neuronal firing and EEG recordings have been assessed in rats. His research interests cover physiological rhythms related to attention, arousal, and consciousness in both the central and peripheral nervous systems, with a focus on understanding mental states.

Meet the Volume Editor

Paul Robinson is a Professor in the Medical Division at University College London. He has co-written or co-edited books on Community Treatment of Eating Disorders (2006), Severe and Enduring Eating Disorders (2009), Critical Care for Anorexia Nervosa (2015) and Mentalization-Based Therapy for Eating Disorders (MBT-ED) (2019). He authored Medical Emergencies in Eating Disorders (MEED), 2022 and the website meed. org. uk. He has published over 80 peer-reviewed papers. In 2012, he launched an MSc degree course based in the UCL Division of Medicine in Eating Disorders and Clinical Nutrition, the only one of its kind. He is editor in chief of "Eating Disorders, a Comprehensive International View", published by Springer Nature in 2024.

Contents

Preface

This book was conceived as a result of many controversial aspects which have emerged in the clinical practice of eating disorders. These topics include the following: 1. Does severe and enduring eating disorder (SEED) actually exist? 2. Can anorexia nervosa ever be treated with palliative care? 3. Can online treatment of eating disorders ever replace in-person treatment? 4. Why do patients with anorexia nervosa get osteoporosis, and how can it be treated? 5. Can exercise be a treatment for eating disorders? 6. How does the study of mentalizing help us understand eating disorders? 7. Can bariatric surgery be used in people with obesity? 8. How are obesity and eating disorders associated?

Readers of the book will find that these questions are addressed, although final answers are often elusive. Does severe and enduring eating disorder (SEED) actually exist? The chapter by Bradshaw et al. examines SEED, suggesting that despite its challenging definition, the concept is deemed valid by clinicians, albeit with notable downsides. Can anorexia nervosa ever be treated with palliative care? This important question is also addressed in a chapter by Dr. Bradshaw et al, who point to several cases in the UK in which patients who have had repeated episodes of forced feeding, sometimes leading to them being traumatized, have gone to court, and it has been agreed that they should not be force-fed in the future. This has led to intense controversy with accusations that services have "given up" on patients with chronic illness. Can online treatment of eating disorders ever replace in-person treatment?

Authors Vogel and Gill report how, in Chile, with limited clinical services, patients with anorexia nervosa were treated using online therapy, which was developed during the COVID pandemic, and weight gain was significant in online patients. Why do patients with anorexia nervosa get osteoporosis, and how can it be treated? Authors Gomez and Pino try to answer these questions. The cause seems to be a combination of low weight, poor diet and hormone changes. However, only weight gain is recommended as a treatment for osteoporosis in anorexia nervosa. Transdermal oestrogen seems to have a beneficial impact on adolescent bone health in anorexia nervosa, and while bisphosphonates do improve bone density, they are not recommended for women of childbearing age because of the potential for teratogenicity. Other treatments, including the contraceptive pill and calcium and Vitamin D supplements, do not appear to work.

Can exercise be a treatment for eating disorders? This novel idea was tested using a powerful technique, a meta-analysis of 7 studies with 473 total participants with binge eating disorder (BED). The results suggest that, somewhat surprisingly, exercise did have an impact on depression and some eating disorder symptoms in BED patients, but there was no effect on binge frequency. The combination of exercise and CBT was better than CBT alone in reducing binge frequency. This finding suggests that a gym room in the treatment of BED might supplement the psychologist's office.

How does the study of mentalizing help us understand eating disorders? Mentalizing is a concept increasingly recognized as important in many conditions, including personality disorders and eating disorders. Dr. Gagliardini and Colli's chapter examines mentalizing and personality in predicting eating pathology.

Research in both areas is quite inconsistent, but a number of conclusions can be reached: Patients with eating disorders and personality disorders tend to have increased chronicity and reduced levels of functioning. Patients with bulimia nervosa can be classified into a poorer functioning, emotionally dysregulated, and a better functioning, perfectionistic group. Regarding mentalizing, the authors report that this ability was reduced in eating disorder patients and that several different patterns of mentalizing can be discerned. Can bariatric surgery be used in people with obesity? The chapter by Dr. Toprak and Toprak documents the positive outcomes for patients with obesity following bariatric surgery. Still, it points out that BED can have a negative effect on the outcome of bariatric surgery. Of course, the definition of binge eating needs to be considered when gastric volume has been reduced surgically, hence limiting the size of any meal, including binges. How are obesity and eating disorders associated? Iakovina Koutoufa tackles this complex matter in her chapter. She looks at how body image problems can be associated with eating disorders in people living with obesity, how dieting, which is generally central in obesity management, can make eating disorders worse, and how the environment, with both obesogenic and stigmatizing characteristics, can complicate recovery in people with both eating disorders and obesity.

Hence, this book gives valuable information on several controversial areas. This does not mean that all controversies in eating disorders are covered, and many other issues remain. For example, how should patients with both eating disorders and Emotionally Unstable Personality Disorders be treated? Both conditions can be life-threatening, but may need different approaches. How should patients with both eating disorders and Autism be treated? What is the place of medication, such as antidepressants or antipsychotics, in the treatment of eating disorders? How should we approach the treatment of the approximately 50% of patients with eating disorders who do not respond satisfactorily to recommended treatment? These questions are among those that could be addressed in a further consideration of controversies in eating disorders.

Paul Robinson
Professor (Teaching),
Division of Medicine,
University College London,
London, United Kingdom

Chapter 1

Perspective Chapter: What's in a Name? The Meanings and Implications of Labels in Eating Disorders

Adaeze Bradshaw, Jess Griffiths, Paul Robinson and Jacinta Tan

Abstract

Effectively treating severe and enduring eating disorders (SEED) can be challenging. The impact on quality of life for those with severe and enduring eating disorder is often severe, yet ambivalence towards accepting recommended treatments can be problematic. At the same time, risk to life can result in escalating conflict and increasing use of compulsory treatment to the extent of nasogastric tube feeding under restraint or feeding under general anaesthesia. Compulsory treatment, particularly with high levels of restriction for prolonged periods of time, is fraught with ethical, legal and clinical challenges. Complex presentations of severe and enduring eating disorders with comorbidities are becoming more commonplace and may account for the increasing number of these cases to the Court of Protection for authorisation of ceilings of care or withdrawal of active treatment. At the same time, there have been recent proposals of the concept of 'terminal anorexia' which have provoked much controversy around notions of futility in eating disorders. These, along with palliative care and end of life are challenging issues addressed in the chapter. The chapter concludes with suggestions to achieve clarity and resolve some of the conflations and confusions around SEED patients. It suggests that the term 'terminal' is neither helpful nor constructive in the context of eating disorders and should not be used; and that palliative care should be accepted as a holistic approach which is fully compatible with active treatment and can be helpful for many people with SEED.

Keywords: severe and enduring eating disorders, severe and enduring anorexia nervosa (SE-AN), longstanding eating disorders (LSED), compulsory treatment, feeding under restraint, feeding under sedation, palliative care, end of life, court of protection, ethics and law

> *'I certainly believed that unless we kept the patient alive, there was no chance, you know, a dead patient.... who can they talk to? If we could keep them alive, there could be a moment when they felt they could discuss how they were feeling.' (P3)*

> *'The only thing we achieved was keeping her alive, she had no life. It's preserving life for life's sake. What we were doing was effectively torturing her.' (P4) [1]*

1. Introduction

In this chapter we tackle some of the most controversial issues that have emerged in the field of eating disorders. Some of the questions we try to address are:

1. If a patient has had a severe eating disorder for many years, is it useful to think about that patient in a different way compared to a person with a very short history?

2. If a patient refuses treatment for an eating disorder, is it ethical to enforce treatment to save that person's life?

3. If a patient has had several attempts at refeeding under coercion and they ask the clinician not to repeat the coercion in the future, should the clinician agree, if it appears to be in the best interests of the patient?

4. What if any is the role of the courts in making these decisions?

2. SEED: What use is it?

The idea of a severe eating disorder lasting a long time is not new. Borson and Katon (p. 264) [2] describe the many medical complications of chronic anorexia nervosa (AN). Strober [3] describes a constellation of features in chronic AN and states (p. 246) "the person with chronic anorexia nervosa shuns affection or compassionate understanding. The plight of the chronically ill—a life existentially bleak, a body frail and debilitated—is heart rending." Yager [4] described chronic eating disorders and included longstanding, intractable bulimia nervosa (BN) as well as AN. Robinson [5] coined the term "severe and enduring eating disorder" (SEED) and described patients with anorexia nervosa of long duration with high levels of comorbidity and need for complex care. The characteristics of SEED included severity, requiring the care of several members of a multidisciplinary team, with repeated admissions to inpatient or day care and relapse after discharge, and duration, with several years of uninterrupted illness. Symptoms were not only rooted in the eating disorder, with low weight, bulimia, vomiting, and laxative abuse, but also affective, with depression and anxiety, social isolation, as well as occupational, with unemployment, financial hardship, and family stress. These numerous symptoms profoundly affected quality of life (QoL) and a comparison with other severe and enduring mental illnesses, such as schizophrenia, revealed comparable impact on quality of life. The idea for SEED was sparked by a particular patient, a 34-year-old male, with bulimia and anorexia nervosa since the age of 18. He had spent about half of the previous 16 years in hospital and nearly died several times. He required help with a housing problem and to access social work he needed to be referred to the Community Mental Health Team (CMHT). After he was referred the response came back "We cannot accept this referral because the patient does not have a severe and enduring mental illness (SEMI)." This suggested that chronic severe anorexia nervosa could not be classified as a severe and enduring mental illness and this discovery led to the publication of a book "Severe and Enduring Eating Disorders" in 2009 [5].

SEED can be compared with the idea of severe and enduring mental illness. As can be seen from the case study mentioned above, the diagnoses included in serious and enduring mental illness have tended to focus on psychotic disorders, in general schizophrenia, bipolar disorder and some recurrent depression [6]. Stuart [6] suggested that this list should also include long standing nonpsychotic disorders such as eating disorders. In general psychiatry, a case has been made that the focus on symptom removal does not cover the broad range of difficulties experienced by people with chronic mental illness, and the idea of the Recovery approach was developed in which improved quality of life, rather than symptom reduction, is the aim [6, 7]. The validity and usefulness of SEED as a concept has been challenged in several ways. Raykos et al. [8] showed that improvement in patients with Anorexia Nervosa treated with CBT appeared unrelated to severity or length of history. Downs et al. [9] argue that poor outcome from eating disorders is more related to unavailability of adequate treatment, than intrinsic characteristics of the illnesses. This relates more to treatment shortcomings than the question of whether SEED exists or not. However, although clinicians mostly agree that they have met many patients with SEED [10], the concept seems to evaporate when closely studied. Wildes et al. [11] using structural equation mixture modelling found no evidence of a SEED subgroup in a large group of patients.

Moreover, Bamford et al. [12] found no evidence that a focus on quality of life, rather than weight and eating disorder symptoms, resulted in benefit for patients with longstanding eating disorders. Then there is issue of prognosis. The view that using the term SEED about a patient means that the clinician thinks that the patient will always have the disorder is wrong. Anyone who has been in the field for a few years will have met patients with very long illnesses who made complete recoveries. Steinhausen's [13] study of the prognosis of anorexia nervosa showed that the longer the duration of follow up, the higher the complete recovery rate. Lastly, the acronym SE-AN suggests that we are just talking about anorexia nervosa. However, clinical practice shows that longstanding bulimia nervosa can also be severe and enduring [14].

Nevertheless, the experience of clinicians suggests that the category reflects patients they treat, and that the idea of SEED should be retained. There is no agreed definition of SEED, but it has been suggested [15] that the following might form part of such a definition: 1. Severity: the condition has major impacts on physical and mental health and social function; 2. Duration: The condition has endured for several years. The exact duration is uncertain, but 3 years has been suggested as a time beyond which recovery becomes more difficult [16] and 7 years was used in a randomised trial of therapy for SE-AN (Severe and Enduring Anorexia Nervosa) [17]; 3. Limited response to evidence-based treatment. This could be failure to respond to such treatment or repeated relapse following episodes of treatment. There is further uncertainty whether we should be referring to total duration of illness, duration of illness since becoming an adult, or duration of receiving a range of high-quality treatments, when trying to develop a definition of SEED. SEED as a term may be unhelpfully emotive, and some people now prefer the term long standing eating disorder (LSED) which is perceived as more neutral with respect to past treatment and current severity. Whether or not we can identify the SEED group of patients statistically, their management continues to give rise to difficult questions that we need to address:

1. Can we predict a poor outcome when we are assessing patients with eating disorders? Identified factors in a poor prognosis vary between studies, but the list include: adult onset, symptom severity, autism, longer duration of illness prior to the initial contact, vomiting, bulimia, and purgative abuse, chronicity of illness, and obsessive-compulsive personality symptoms [13, 18–22].

2. For patients with longstanding eating disorders who have had several episodes of the best available treatment is it reasonable in the light of Bamford et al. [12] to concentrate on quality of life rather than continuing to try and influence weight and other eating disorder features?

3. For patients with longstanding eating disorders who have had several unhelpful episodes of involuntary care, should we have a different attitude to compulsion?

4. Is there ever a place for palliative or end of life care or assisted dying if it is legally permitted [23]?

It is easy to pose questions but less easy to provide answers. We should say first that this is an area in which both evidence and clinical practice are developing. However, there are some relevant sources to cite.

It is important to understand that the evidence base in this area is very scant, and furthermore what evidence we do have about treatments and their efficacy in eating disorders in general may not apply in longstanding, complex and/or severe forms of eating disorders. The hierarchy of quality of evidence used in guidance such as NICE is illustrated in **Figure 1**. Most of the evidence in relation to SEED is from level IV, i.e. expert opinion which although respected is the least reliable level of evidence. In this chapter we have made several points and as far as possible have illustrated each one with support from the literature.

The complex and interrelated factors which contribute towards clinical decision making in the case of a severely ill patient with an eating disorder are outlined in **Figure 2**. The lack of robust evidence for the treatment of longstanding eating disorders (outlined above) may result in a stronger reliance on clinician and team's own beliefs and values about the illness, potentially impacting the clinical decision-making process. These differing views were outlined by participant quotes at the beginning of this chapter, highlighting how some clinicians may feel that continued treatment is necessary for life preservation, whilst others identify the potential for it to cause iatrogenic harm. The most significant factors impacting upon clinical decision making related to the external processes impacting upon clinicians and services, these factors are listed within the figure below [1, 25].

We provide treatment to people with eating disorders, sometimes against their will, and practices such as forced nasogastric feeding are applied at all stages of the illnesses, mainly for patients with anorexia nervosa, both children and adults [26]. However, should this practice continue indefinitely especially if it is proving

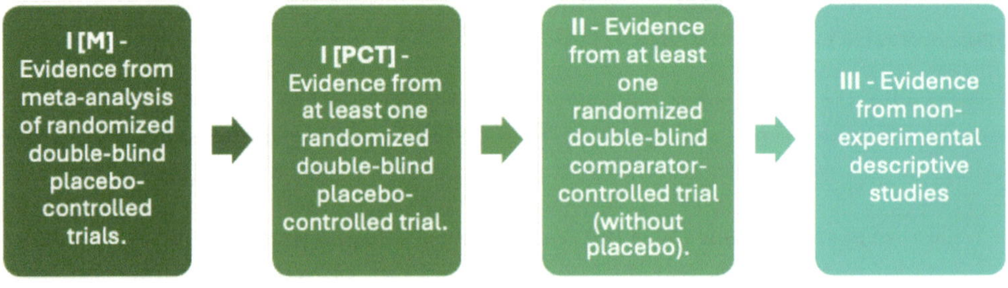

Figure 1.
Adapted from Ottawa illustrating the most reliable sources of evidence to the left, and less reliable to the right [24].

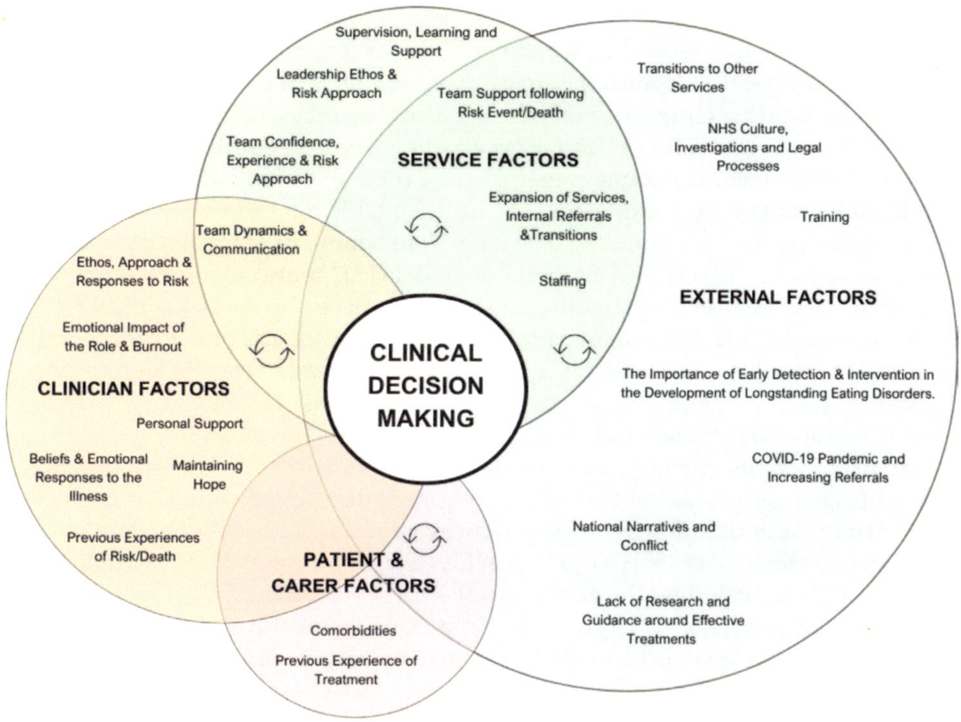

Figure 2.
A schematic depiction of the complexity of factors involved in clinical decision making in the case of a severely ill patient with an eating disorder [1].

ineffective and causing suffering to the patient? The SEED concept may have some relevance here. It is patients with a long illness who have had repeated failed attempts at compulsory refeeding, who sometimes ask services not to repeat this procedure in the future. They would clearly come under the SEED rubric. The English Court of Protection has considered some of these situations and in many cases has agreed for compulsory treatment to be avoided in the future [27]. The cited paper reports "All of the five cases involved female patients over the age of 18 who had suffered from Anorexia Nervosa for more than 14 years." The Court of Protection has subsequently been involved in similar cases and has ruled in one that although the patient lacked capacity to accept or reject treatment, her best interests were served by her not being subject to compulsory treatment [28].

3. Compulsory treatment for presentations for severe and enduring ED (SEED)

People with eating disorders are often ambivalent to treatment, and more so in those with SEED. This then immediately raises an ethical dilemma for healthcare professionals—if someone is not agreeing to treatment, when is it ethically justified to use compulsion, that is, treatment imposed without patient consent, and for how long is it justified?

The ethics of enforcing treatment becomes even more fraught when patients decline interventions for lifesaving and/or life-threatening presentations. There is a body of evidence that suggests a different approach to compulsion should be adopted for those that have had several treatment episodes of involuntary care.

Compulsory treatment continues to bring up various ethical, legal and clinical dilemmas for treating clinicians not least because they may find their duty of care to save the patient by providing effective treatment is in direct conflict with their ethical obligation to support the patient in maintaining their autonomy when made by an individual with capacity. Compulsion can be acceptable for a short period of time to enable lifesaving intervention [29]. The long-term benefit of extended compulsory treatment remains unclear [30] though Zohar-Beja [31] found that both short- and long-term use of compulsory treatment can be beneficial. No study has been found to conclude that a deterioration in patient-clinician therapeutic relationship occurs because of compulsory treatment. Garner [32] recommended certain factors that maintained neutrality and can improve relationship. These included establishment of genuine therapeutic alliance and engaging the family and loved one.

Extended periods of compulsory treatment are controversial amongst psychiatrists and other clinicians involved in the treatment of eating disorders. It is established that those with SEED have lower than average quality of life. The provision of the Mental Health Act (MHA) [33] provides a legal framework for treatment of mental disorders, including the whole spectrum of eating disorders [34]. Goldner, [35] advocated a series of strategies that facilitates less use of coercive or compulsion in treatment. These include identifying reasons for refusal, promoting autonomy and involving the family. Goldner writes "*Chronic illness may indicate a particularly resistant form of anorexia nervosa and may follow repeated attempts at treatment. It may be inappropriate to approach treatment of the chronic anorexic patient with a zealous or aggressive plan of intervention*" [35] (p. 304).

3.1 Clinical ethics

The Four principles of clinical ethics that underpin ethical decisional making in clinical practice [36] are outlined below in **Figure 3**.

3.2 Beneficence

The health professional's main role is to care for their patient's health and wellbeing. This includes times when health professionals act to protect the patient's health and wellbeing against their will, for example, when using the MHA [33].

3.3 Non-maleficence

Despite the clinician's ability to help patients, there is obligation on the clinician not to cause harm to patients. Harm takes various forms including iatrogenic harm, from psychological therapies, side effects from medication and use of compulsion to compel treatment. Therefore, potential harms of any treatment or non-treatment must be weighed against potential benefits and can only be justified if the potential harms are outweighed by the potential benefits.

3.4 Justice

The distribution of resources should be considered in ethical decision making. Such resources include, workforce, clinical estates (such as therapy rooms, clinic

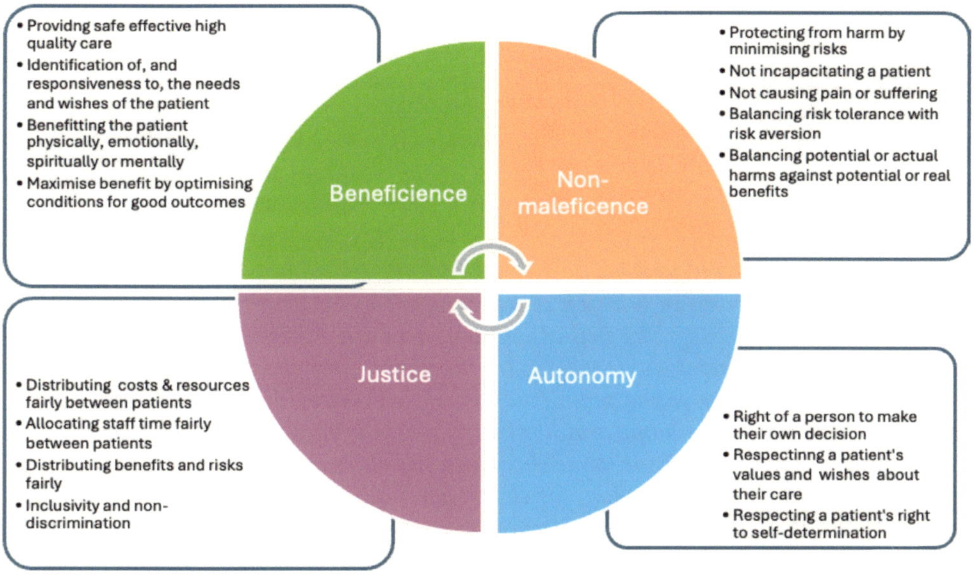

Figure 3.
The four principles of clinical ethics [36], depiction by Adaeze Bradshaw.

rooms, hospital beds) and financial outlay (such as costs incurred in prescribing, tests monitoring, referrals to national centres and to admission to units outside of region). It is a useful reminder that all interventions have an impact on other patients in terms of equitable distribution of resources, and that in the real world the most beneficent option may not always be feasible nor available nor just to others. Justice also demands that healthcare services are inclusive, and patients are treated fairly and not discriminated against, because of any personal characteristics such as race, ethnicity, gender, age or diagnosis.

3.5 Autonomy

Wherever possible, the ability of the patient to make their own decisions about their care and their future should be encouraged. The Montgomery judgement clarifies that patients' values and views with regard to what matters to them should be taken into account in determining the information that should be provided to aid their decision making in obtaining informed consent [37]. Consideration should also be given to the impact of relationships and circumstances on their ability to make autonomous decisions. The code of practice of the Mental Capacity Act [38] requires that clinicians support patient autonomy and patients' wishes as far as possible, even if capacity is lacking.

3.6 Ethical decision-making in the treatment of SEED

Health care professionals are trained to use their knowledge and skills in caring for their patients. Increasingly, as eating disorder presentations become ever more complex, decision making is becoming correspondingly more difficult and complex. There are notable ethical decision-making tools to support clinicians in navigating these difficult terrains [39].

The following vignette illustrates the ethical complexity of some SEED cases, it is a fictional composite based on real experiences:

Rachel is a 20-year-old woman with a history since age 11 of severe anorexia nervosa. She had been sexually abused as a child. She was admitted to a child and adolescent eating disorders service and refused to eat or drink. She was fed by nasogastric (NG) tube which had to be inserted against her will and she was treated under a compulsory order (the English Mental Health Act). She was discharged at a better but still low weight and was stable for several years. However, at age 16 she lost weight again and was readmitted and fed by NG tube under restraint. She described post-traumatic stress symptoms in relation to her childhood abuse and to the traumatic effects of forced NG feeding. She was also diagnosed with Autistic Spectrum Disorder. Her weight increased but she was still under the normal range, and she went to a residential placement for young people with eating disorders. Her parents felt they could not cope with her at home and her illness was having a negative influence on her younger sister. In the residential home she began self-harming and vomiting and she required several medical admissions for electrolyte stabilisation. This continued until she was 18 and the residential home decided she was too severely ill for them, whereupon she was transferred to a hospital. In hospital she complained of epigastric pain whenever she was fed, and the feeding route was changed to a naso-jejunal tube. She interfered with the feeding tube and her BMI could not be raised above 11.5. Eating disorder units were unable to take her at that BMI and the options discussed on the medical ward were:

1. *Keep her long term in the medical ward.*

2. *Keep trying to increase her weight.*

3. *Discharge her to independent accommodation with daily nursing visits.*

Downs et al. [9] have argued that better treatment would change the course of the illness. This is unlikely in the case above. Clinicians need guidance on how to help someone in this precarious state. One option not considered by this clinical team has been proposed by others, that is deeply sedating the patient and delivering NG feeding in an Intensive Care Unit [40]. This raises many practical and ethical questions, which we will address later in this chapter. These issues are very difficult to resolve and need to be discussed openly and honestly between clinical and legal staff and patients and their carers.

When the patient is under 18, the approach seems rather different to that in adults. No patients under 18 (the age of legal majority in England and Wales) have been presented to the Court of Protection, and this may be because parental consent can be used for treatment of legal minors. Furthermore, for developmental reasons we would not consider patients under the age of 18 as part of the SEED group.

Offering care which does not include the use of compulsory treatment when the patient is refusing refeeding bears a resemblance to palliative care, as the treatment which is most likely to improve health and prolong life is not being provided and death is a likely consequence. This does present a difficult dilemma for the clinical staff. There is an argument for cases in which this approach is considered should be referred to the relevant court.

4. SEED and the court of protection[1]

This complexity in presentations and healthcare professionals' emerging trends to address them through the Court of Protection (CoP) following years of extended compulsory treatment to no significant success are noted. Cave and Tan [27] explored the first five cases of 'eating disorders in extremis', that is, where there was severe risk to life yet no clear solution, that were heard at the CoP from 2012 to 2017. They concluded with multiple recommendations including ensuring a patient-centred-approach to decision-making rather than clinician-centred-approach and the need to broaden the base of clinical expert witnesses in use by the court. Since then, 11 [11] further cases involving eating disorders have been heard by the Court of Protection (personal communication, Alex Ruck-Keene). Several articles have highlighted the perceived pressure and informal coercion in this patient population [41, 42]. However, this is difficult to identify in the 12 Court of Protection cases since 2017, where the issue has mainly been making decisions about whether the person has capacity to refuse treatment, and what options remain after extensive treatment. It will be useful for future learning and research to undertake detailed exploration of the types and complexities of the cases from 2017 to present, to explore any emerging themes and absence or presence of any practical strategies to help resolve dilemmas prior to recourse to the courts.

The first five Court of Protection cases have established that patients who have LSED (SEED) can lack capacity, which is consistent with previous research [27, 43–45]. The law allows treatment decisions to be made in a patient's best interests if they lack capacity [38]. However, best interests require balancing benefit against harm for each individual. Hospital admissions remove people from their homes and communities and focus almost exclusively on the mental illness, which can further narrow the already narrowed focus of people with eating disorders. Admissions, particularly for compulsory treatment, can be experienced as a restrictive loss of freedom. Inpatient treatment for eating disorders, particularly if compulsory, require that patients comply with prescribed diet plans aiming to restore weight, which can be experienced as very controlling. If patients struggle to eat enough, they may be offered nasogastric tube feeding. If they then refuse this, even more restrictive measures may be used, such as nasogastric feeding under restraint, which involves passing a nasogastric tube while holding the patient down. Recent research on

[1] The Court of Protection (England and Wales) makes decisions on financial or welfare matters for people who cannot make decisions at the time they need to be made (they 'lack mental capacity'). They are based in London. Most cases are heard by district judges and a senior judge but can sometimes be heard by High Court judges. Cases can sometimes be transferred to a local court for hearing. The Court of Protection are responsible for:

- deciding whether someone has the mental capacity to make a particular decision for themselves
- appointing deputies to make ongoing decisions for people who lack mental capacity
- giving people permission to make one-off decisions on behalf of someone else who lacks mental capacity
- handling urgent or emergency applications where a decision must be made on behalf of someone else without delay
- making decisions about a lasting power of attorney or enduring power of attorney and considering any objections to their registration
- considering applications to make statutory wills or gifts
- making decisions about when someone can be deprived of their liberty under the Mental Capacity Act

From: https://www.gov.uk/courts-tribunals/court-of-protection, Accessed on 27th March 2025.

nasogastric tube feeding has highlighted how distressing and traumatic this experience can be for patients, their families and staff [26, 46]. A recent audit has shown that this may be done daily for a long period of time for some individuals [26, 47, 48]. And finally, if there is too high a risk in restraint, as might occur with violent struggles or fragile bones, then nasogastric feeding under anaesthesia may be carried out.

4.1 Feeding under general anaesthesia

The use of general anaesthesia is the ultimate loss of autonomy – any patient undergoing anaesthesia is surrendering control of their bodies and awareness to the medical staff around them. To be deprived of this control or awareness without consent and against one's will could be considered the ultimate loss of control or agency. This would be doubly painful in some eating disorders where the paradox of a strong drive to be in control of one's own body and intake, yet experiencing a loss of control over behaviours due to the disorder itself and the attempts of others to make them eat more is often a core issue [48, 49]. Added to that is the impact of the refeeding which would take place during unconsciousness – it would certainly be to a higher weight, though it is not evident whether clinicians would feel that they should only feed sufficiently to get the patient out of danger, or feel that they need to 'go for broke' to achieve a 'healthy weight' during unconsciousness, due to prior difficulties with feeding when conscious? There is no research that we know of about this experience, only anecdote – one of the authors was told by a research participant that she awoke in a completely different body after anaesthesia for refeeding and was highly traumatised because of the shock and alienation. In addition, the Open Justice website,[2] accessed 6th March 2025, corroborated the lack of evidence and research in this area: "we have searched and not found, evidence-based research and professional guidelines about re-feeding anorexic patients in induced comas under general anaesthesia".

Our identities and sense of the self are embodied, and the relationship that people with eating disorders have with their own bodies is complex. There can be a toxic love of the thin ideal [50]. Stanghellini and colleagues [51] developed a questionnaire for identity and eating disorders (IDEA), which extracted four factors, relating to the following phenomena: 'feeling oneself only through the gaze of the other and defining oneself only through the evaluation of the other', 'feeling oneself only through objective measures', 'feeling extraneous from one's own body', and 'feeling oneself through starvation' [51].

Sudden changes in one's body can be difficult even with informed consent, as evidenced by the well-known impact of a mastectomy on women with breast cancer. Research suggests that there is a range of emotional reactions post-mastectomy as well as a need to renegotiate identity and relationships with their own bodies when women undergo a mastectomy [37, 52, 53]. Mastectomies, however, are fully consenting surgeries, where the women are advised about their options and can consider the potential changes to their bodies during the informed consent process. There is a need to examine the impact of awaking to a changed body when patients have lived in their underweight bodies for a long time and have no opportunity to experience and adapt to their changed bodies over time as refeeding proceeds.

Unfortunately, we have insufficient evidence of the long-term harms of what appears to be an increasing use of highly restrictive practices such as nasogastric tube

[2] Promoting Open Justice; Anorexic teenager in 10-day induced coma for re-feeding: What next? – Promoting Open Justice in the Court of Protection.

feeding under restraint and refeeding under anaesthesia and must consider with care the potential short- and long-term impact of the use of coercion.

5. End of life, palliative care and terminal eating disorders: Disentangling the labels and aiming for respectful discourse

When discussing severe eating disorders where sufferers, their families and treatment teams feel that they are running out of viable options, some terms tend to be used loosely and interchangeably: 'end of life', 'palliative care', 'futility', 'terminal eating disorders'. These terms raise considerable anxiety and conflict, because of their perceived meanings and implications which evoke strong emotions. This section will attempt to disentangle and consider them.

It must be stressed that most people who have LSED do not face end of life issues. **Figure 4** illustrates the possible range of categories in which people may suffer from a longstanding or enduring disorder may fall, and furthermore people can dynamically move from one category to another. It is only the fourth and smallest subgroup of individuals who are experiencing acutely challenging situations that raise serious questions of whether treatment is futile, evoking despair in themselves, their loved ones, support networks, and treating clinicians [39].

The discussion of end-of-life issues should be conducted in a respectful and unemotive way. As a review of literature concludes, "the debate around end-of-life care in anorexia nervosa needs consented, coherent terminology whose value base is reduced to a minimum and made transparent." This section will attempt to do precisely that.

5.1 The notion of 'end of life'

The Cambridge Dictionary [49] defines 'end-of-life' as: "End-of-life issues relate to someone's death and the time just before it, when it is known that they are likely to die soon from an illness or condition".

This definition gives us a clue of the difficulty involved – it tells us that 'end of life issues' occur when death is 'likely' but does not give precise definitions nor indication

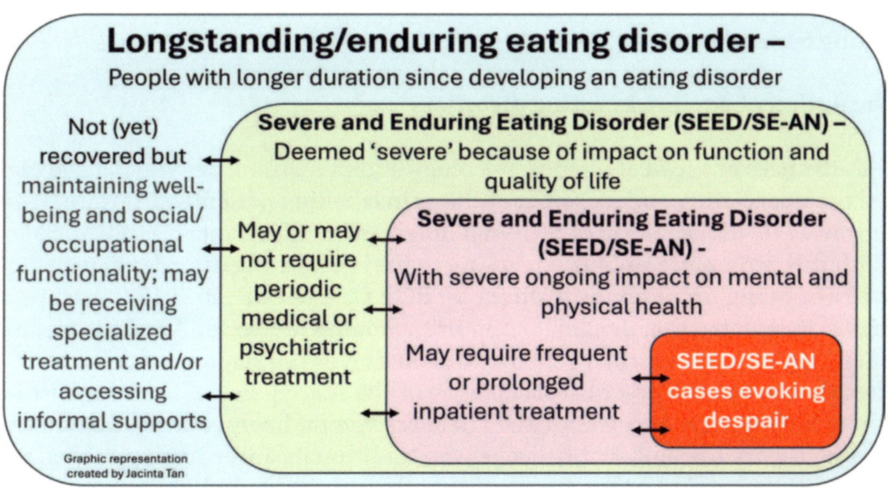

Figure 4.
Different and conceptually distinct subgroups related to SEED/SE-AN [39], created by Jacinta Tan.

of what 'likely' means. There is, on investigation, considerable variation of definition amongst organisations which routinely offer end of life care. The Marie Curie cancer charity [54] tells us that "End of life care involves treatment, care and support for people who are thought to be in the last year of life." However, the National Institute for Health and Care Excellence (NICE) guideline NG142 [55] says: "This guideline covers organising and delivering end of life care services, which provide care and support in the final weeks and months of life (or for some conditions, years), and the planning and preparation for this." And finally, the National Health Service [56] in the United Kingdom says: "End of life care is support for people who are in the last months or years of their life."

End of life is, therefore, best understood as the final phase of a person's life. The anticipated cause of death is not specified, and the duration of remaining life is also unclear.

5.2 The notion of terminal illness

'Terminal illness' is defined as an incurable or irreversible illness. The NHS [57] says: "There's no right or wrong way to feel when you're told you have a terminal illness, which is a health condition that cannot be cured and you'd most likely die from." This underlines the lack of a time frame and adds the notion of inability to recover.

A terminal illness therefore is one where death will eventually result, yet death may take many years to occur after onset or diagnosis. Dementia is currently a terminal illness, yet death is unlikely for many years particularly with the advent of drugs which slow progression, and with advances of science death from dementia may soon no longer be inevitable. The notion of 'terminal illness' is therefore neither precise nor particularly helpful. A more useful and less emotive term that should be used is 'life-limiting illness', which indicates an illness likely to end in death but is agnostic about how long more the patient will live or whether the illness would actually kill them.

As well as understanding that our terminology suggests we cannot pin down whether and when an illness would end in death, we should note that research suggests physicians are poor at prognosticating time left to live. Physicians identify with confidence when a patient has more than a year of life remaining and equally have confidence in identifying when death is imminent; but have only a 32% accuracy in predicting 6 months to live [58].

5.3 The notion of staging in eating disorders

The advances of medical science, oncology and palliative care, which have highlighted the uncertainty and lack of usefulness in labelling patients as 'terminal', are moving away from the notion of terminal illness in conditions such as advanced cancer. With this general trend, it is intriguing to find that eating disorder debate appears to have been going in the opposite direction in the last decade. In 2015, Treasure and colleagues postulated that evidence supports a Staging Model for Anorexia Nervosa [59]. See **Figure 5** [59] for their schematic depiction of the staging model.

There has been little practical acceptance of the staging model in eating disorder treatment by healthcare professionals. There are several likely reasons. The first is that the staging theory uncomfortably evokes the traditional cancer staging model, where it is widely assumed that 'Stage 4 cancer' is both untreatable and indicates end-of-life—an expectation which is now increasingly confounded by recent advances such as immunotherapy [60, 61]. The second is that eating disorder services rarely see

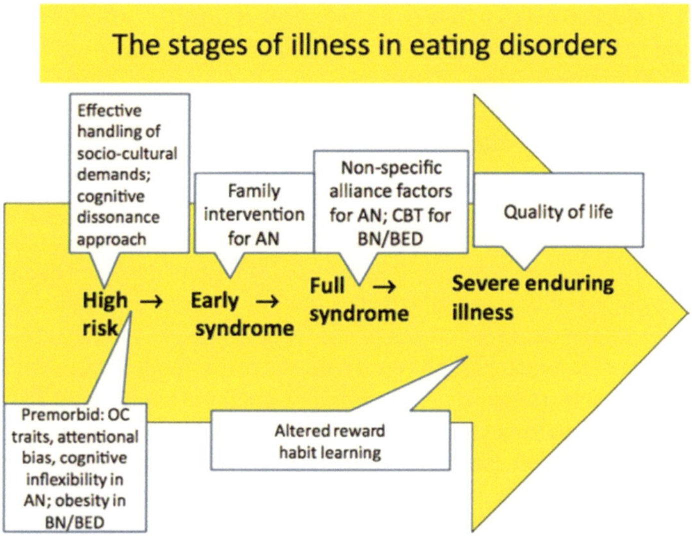

Figure 5.
The stages of illness in eating disorders [59].

people at the two earlier 'high risk' or 'early syndrome' stages of eating disorders, despite growing evidence of cost effectiveness and quality-adjusted life years savings of prevention and prompt early intervention [62, 63]. Instead, current eating disorder health services currently focus treatment resources on the 'full syndrome' and 'severe enduring illness' stages, which the model suggests are the least amenable to treatment. The third is unlike many cancers, there are no universal preventative or public health programmes that aim to reduce risk or ameliorate the high-risk stages [62, 64], enabling prompt and curative treatment. And the fourth is a deep discomfort with abandoning the aim of recovery for eating disorders at any stage [65].

In the last 3 years, there has been considerable, highly emotive controversy around Gaudiani and colleagues' proposal of the concept of 'terminal anorexia' [42, 66–68]. In coining 'terminal anorexia', Gaudiani and colleagues clearly use 'terminal' as indicating several things—imminent death, futility of treatment, and irreversible illness. The controversy basically centres around whether there is an end stage to severe eating disorders and, if so, how to identify it; whether we can accept futility and predict death from eating disorders; whether our notions of futility may reflect poor treatment options and resources; and whether, in consequence, it is ethical or acceptable to contemplate treatment plans which do not aim for recovery [69].

5.4 The notions of palliative care and life limiting illness

The World Health Organisation defines palliative care as follows: "Palliative care is an approach that improves the quality of life of patients and their families facing the problems associated with life-threatening illness, through the prevention and relief of suffering by means of early identification and impeccable assessment, and treatment of pain and other problems – physical, psychosocial and spiritual" [70].

Marie Curie [71] says: "After you get a terminal diagnosis, you can have palliative care at any stage in your illness. You can also have palliative care alongside treatments, therapies and medicines aimed at controlling your illness, such as chemotherapy or radiotherapy." They also clarify that palliative care is not the same as end-of-life care: "Although it can include end of life care, palliative care is much broader and can last for longer. Having palliative care doesn't necessarily mean that you're likely to die soon – some people have palliative care for years."

This concept of palliative care is crucially important—that it is a holistic service focusing on optimising function and quality of life, that can go alongside more active specialist treatment for patients with life limiting illnesses and their families and therefore is not just applicable at the end of life. In the eating disorder context, where there is severe suffering and loss of quality of life, palliative care has been much misunderstood and conflated with medical futility. Palliative care has further been misunderstood by some eating disorder clinicians as the alternative to any active treatment, with care being transferred to palliative care teams for 'a good death'. Unsurprisingly offering palliative care is interpreted by some patients and families as abandonment by eating disorder teams and/or a statement of 'un-treatability' and futility. For example, the Royal College of Psychiatrists (United Kingdom) released a statement on eating disorder patients being offered palliative care which appears to exhibit this conflation and confusion of the role of palliative care: "It's troubling to learn that eating disorder patients have been offered palliative care [..] we would be deeply concerned if this started to be considered clinical practice for anorexia nervosa, for which treatment can help individuals recover. While some patients are less responsive to treatment than others, that does not mean they cannot recover now or in the future" [72].

5.5 The role of active treatment and its limitations

The treatment of severe eating disorders includes the use of inpatient admissions, compulsory treatment, and feeding under restraint. It also includes talking therapies such as those well described in the NICE guidelines (2017). These approaches can undoubtedly be helpful, preserve life and can lead to recovery even in the most severely ill patients. Treatment escalation, illustrated in **Figure 6** has its place in the treatment of eating disorders [25]. In this approach, treatments that have been tried and not helped are replaced by either alternative treatments at the same level (for example, CBT-E is provided but is not helpful enough, so is replaced by MANTRA) or

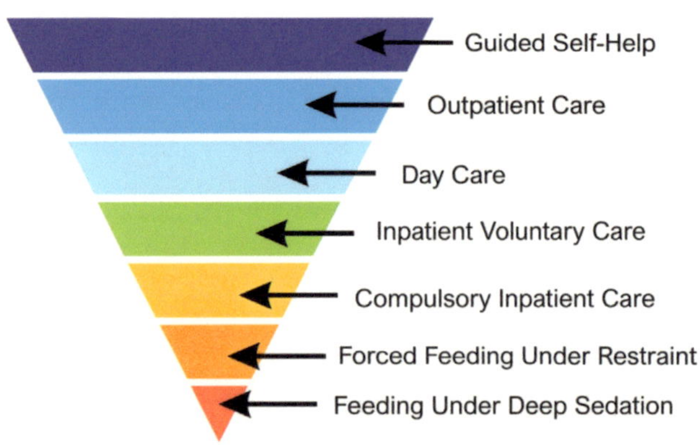

Figure 6.
Treatment of eating disorders, with least restrictive approaches at the top, and treatment becoming increasingly coercive towards the lower part of the figure (depiction by Paul Robinson).

at more coercive levels (for example, voluntary inpatient care is replaced by compulsory inpatient care).

Much as such approaches have their place, there is evidence that the use of coercion, restrictive practices and even talking therapies, which run counter to the drives and compulsions of the eating disorder, can be traumatising [34, 46, 73]. The polarised arguments of active or coercive treatment aiming for recovery versus palliative care aiming for symptom control and quality of life without hope of recovery are unhelpful and need to be more nuanced. The emphasis should shift to minimising suffering and ensuring the optimal outcome for each patient and family, particularly for those with longstanding and severe eating disorders [74]. This balance will shift dynamically depending on myriad patient, family, treatment, and clinician factors, including the development of new treatments and approaches. This is not an area of medicine in which clear therapeutic rules can be laid down. There are certainly some patients in which continued feeding under restraint can be traumatising and may not be in the patient's best interests, following the ethical principle of nonmaleficence [75]. Decisions in such cases rest with the clinical team, the patient and family and sometimes the questions may be deliberated in a court of law, especially when there is difference of opinion [27].

5.6 Resolving the conflations of meaning

To achieve clarity and initiate respectful and meaningful discussions, it is important in mental health to learn from the disciplines of oncology and palliative care and to understand the conversations about end of life in a less emotive way.

To summarise, there is confusion and conflation between 'end of life' and 'terminal illness'. Similarly, palliative care is often mistakenly assumed to only be the alternative to active treatment, and equally mistakenly assumed signal the end-of-life stage of illness. **Figure 7** shows a suggested conceptual understanding of the relationship between the terms.

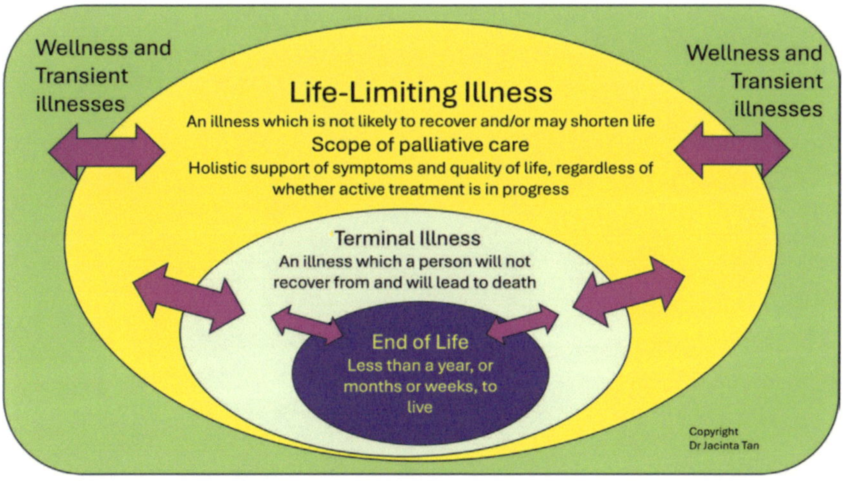

Figure 7.
The scope of palliative care, life limiting illness, terminal illness and the end of life and their relationship to longstanding eating disorders, created by Jacinta Tan.

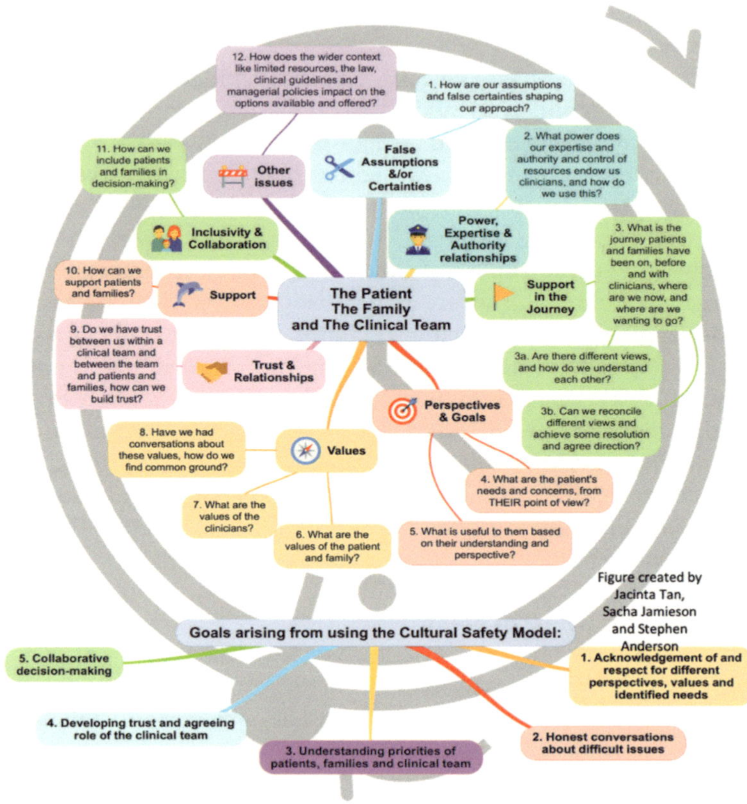

Figure 8.
Cultural Safety model schematic [39] for supporting case conference discussions that are value based and respectful, incorporating all perspectives, created by Jacinta Tan.

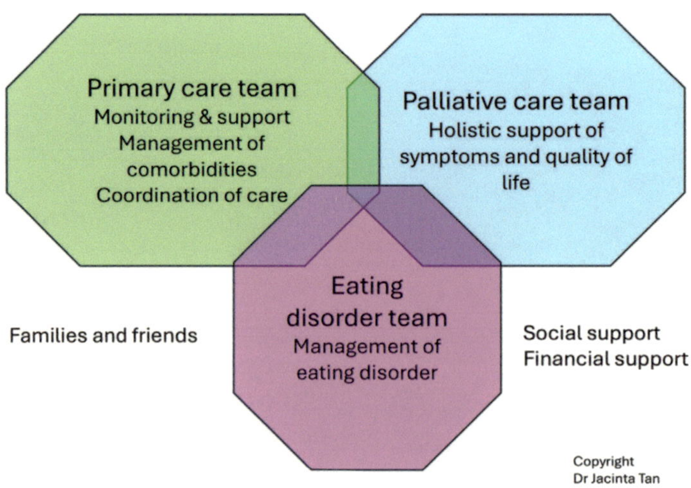

Figure 9.
The possible roles of three different health services for people with long standing eating disorders and their families, created by Jacinta Tan.

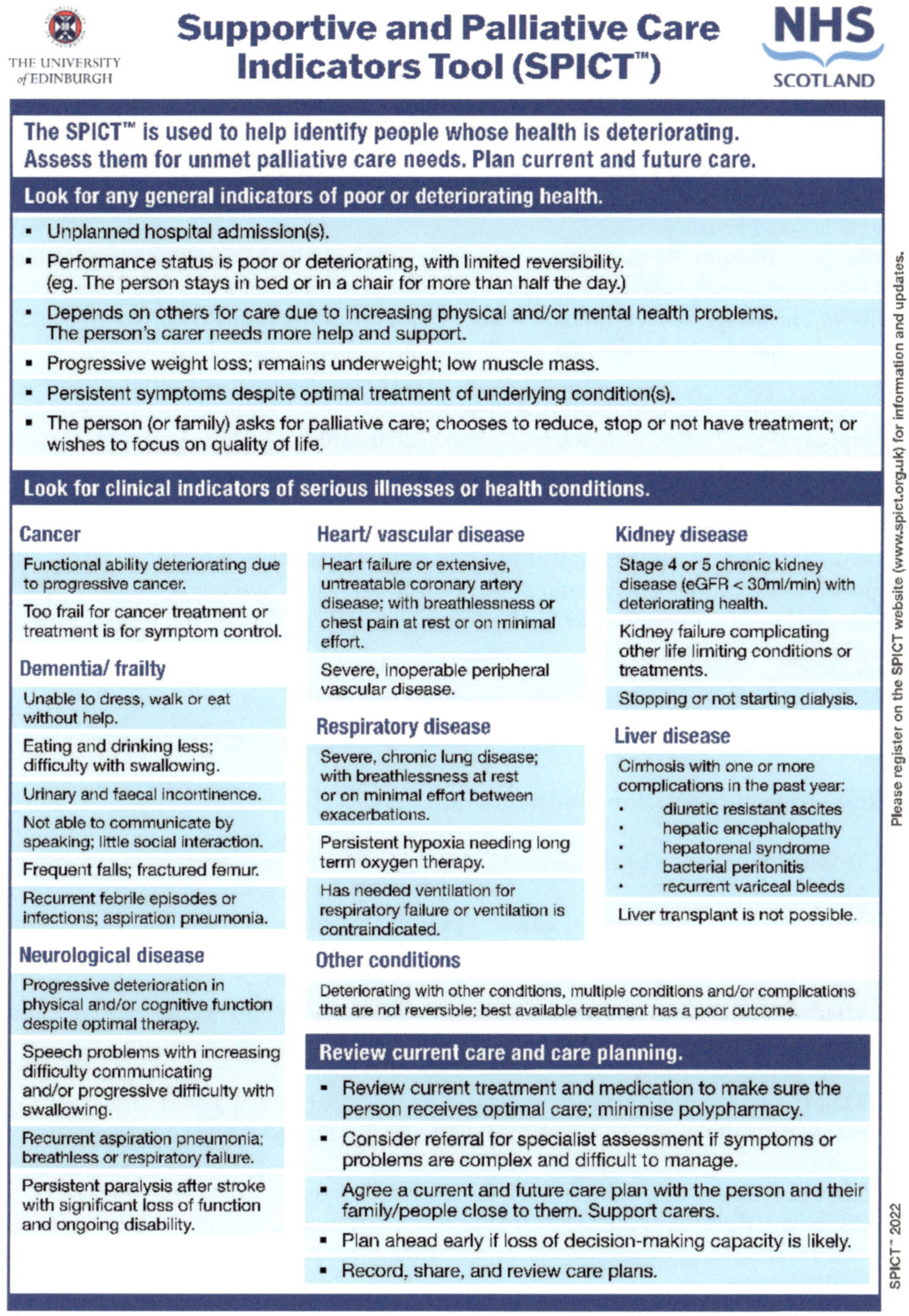

THE UNIVERSITY of EDINBURGH

Supportive and Palliative Care Indicators Tool (SPICT™)

NHS SCOTLAND

The SPICT™ is used to help identify people whose health is deteriorating. Assess them for unmet palliative care needs. Plan current and future care.

Look for any general indicators of poor or deteriorating health.

- Unplanned hospital admission(s).
- Performance status is poor or deteriorating, with limited reversibility. (eg. The person stays in bed or in a chair for more than half the day.)
- Depends on others for care due to increasing physical and/or mental health problems. The person's carer needs more help and support.
- Progressive weight loss; remains underweight; low muscle mass.
- Persistent symptoms despite optimal treatment of underlying condition(s).
- The person (or family) asks for palliative care; chooses to reduce, stop or not have treatment; or wishes to focus on quality of life.

Look for clinical indicators of serious illnesses or health conditions.

Cancer

Functional ability deteriorating due to progressive cancer.

Too frail for cancer treatment or treatment is for symptom control.

Dementia/ frailty

Unable to dress, walk or eat without help.

Eating and drinking less; difficulty with swallowing.

Urinary and faecal incontinence.

Not able to communicate by speaking; little social interaction.

Frequent falls; fractured femur.

Recurrent febrile episodes or infections; aspiration pneumonia.

Neurological disease

Progressive deterioration in physical and/or cognitive function despite optimal therapy.

Speech problems with increasing difficulty communicating and/or progressive difficulty with swallowing.

Recurrent aspiration pneumonia; breathless or respiratory failure.

Persistent paralysis after stroke with significant loss of function and ongoing disability.

Heart/ vascular disease

Heart failure or extensive, untreatable coronary artery disease; with breathlessness or chest pain at rest or on minimal effort.

Severe, inoperable peripheral vascular disease.

Respiratory disease

Severe, chronic lung disease; with breathlessness at rest or on minimal effort between exacerbations.

Persistent hypoxia needing long term oxygen therapy.

Has needed ventilation for respiratory failure or ventilation is contraindicated.

Kidney disease

Stage 4 or 5 chronic kidney disease (eGFR < 30ml/min) with deteriorating health.

Kidney failure complicating other life limiting conditions or treatments.

Stopping or not starting dialysis.

Liver disease

Cirrhosis with one or more complications in the past year:
- diuretic resistant ascites
- hepatic encephalopathy
- hepatorenal syndrome
- bacterial peritonitis
- recurrent variceal bleeds

Liver transplant is not possible.

Other conditions

Deteriorating with other conditions, multiple conditions and/or complications that are not reversible; best available treatment has a poor outcome.

Review current care and care planning.

- Review current treatment and medication to make sure the person receives optimal care; minimise polypharmacy.
- Consider referral for specialist assessment if symptoms or problems are complex and difficult to manage.
- Agree a current and future care plan with the person and their family/people close to them. Support carers.
- Plan ahead early if loss of decision-making capacity is likely.
- Record, share, and review care plans.

Please register on the SPICT website (www.spict.org.uk) for information and updates.

SPICT™ 2022

Figure 10.
The Supportive & Palliative Care Indicators Tool (SPICT) [78], an example of a holistic and multidisciplinary approach to patients at the end of life in the physical health sector. This may be a useful approach for patients with longstanding and severe mental disorders.

When arriving at the stage where a person might have a life-limiting illness and what the best way forward might be, conversations are needed about whether this is a formulation acceptable or useful to all parties involved – clinicians, patients and their families and other loved ones. We recommend employing Cultural Safety principles to have in-depth, open and honest conversations where everyone feels empowered to express their values and wishes, and clinicians also feel empowered to discuss their opinions, recommendations, considerations and constraints with patients and loved ones [39]—see **Figure 8**.

It is also important, if there is a severe and enduring illness, that the focus should shift from treatment alone to include symptom control and holistic improvement of quality of life alongside treatment. To those ends, different teams within healthcare and other agencies should all work together to support patients and their families in their difficult journey. For example, palliative care and primary care clinicians should be involved in the treatment plans for these people to ensure holistic planning of care and support [76]. **Figure 9** illustrates a conceptualisation of possible roles for three different services for individual patients and families.

Where physical health is deteriorating or outcome/recovery is uncertain, there are tools in palliative care that can adapted to be useful for SEED, such as the Supportive and Palliative Care Indicators Tool (SPICT) and the AMBER care bundle, which promote identification of any unmet needs, clear planning, and engagement of the patient and family in advance decision-making [55, 77, 78]. The SPICT [77] is illustrated in **Figure 10**.

6. Conclusions

6.1 Resolution of conflations and confusion

The following are the likely points of broad consensus:

1. That people with severe and enduring eating disorders have a higher long-term morbidity and mortality than the normal population;

2. That treatments can be traumatising and distressing so iatrogenic harm needs to be considered and addressed;

3. That the symptoms, consequences, harms and disability of severe and enduring eating disorders are also severe and distressing, and should be addressed;

4. That despite evidence about the factors which predict a worse outcome, we do not currently have evidence to enable confident prognostication on the individual level about outcome of severe and enduring eating disorders;

5. Palliative care is a holistic approach which is perfectly compatible with active treatment, while being agnostic about how long a patient will live or respond to active eating disorder treatment. Furthermore, utilising palliative care does not imply that the patient has no hope of recovery and can support them to continue with treatment.

Based on the analysis of the issues provided above, we suggest the following:

1. That the term 'terminal' is neither helpful nor constructive in the context of eating disorders and should not be used;

2. That it is possible to agree that a patient likely has a life-limiting disorder (an agreement which is open to revision if they begin to recover) without implying they will die imminently or that they would not benefit from treatment;

3. That all treatment for severe and enduring eating disorders should be tailored to individual need, wishes and context, taking into account past experiences;

4. That Cultural Safety is a good tool to ensure mutual understanding and development of consensus around the way forward for each individual patient and their families, particularly where there are emotive issues or disagreements;

5. That where there is severe and enduring illness, it is likely that co-working between primary care, palliative care and the eating disorder teams would be helpful because it enables alleviating symptoms, improving function and quality of life which is fully compatible with active psychiatric treatment;

6. Where physical health is deteriorating or outcome/recovery is uncertain, we should utilise tools that can assist in ensuring there are no unmet needs and engage patients and families in care planning and advance decision-making [56].

6.2 Holding the tension?

This is a paragraph from one of the authors' thesis [1]:

P1, P5 and P7 spoke about impact of continued and persistent escalated risk, suggesting that clinicians controlling responses to risk leave little space and reflection for treatment decisions that would promote patient resilience and recovery. They referred to this as 'positive risk taking'. P1 explained this, suggesting: 'we can't mollycoddle them, they need rehabilitation to get to the bigger picture (of recovery)' and P5 supported this suggesting that 'one needs to take therapeutic risks in order to create opportunities for recovery'. P7 described how he would 'purposely back off' from patients, describing how he learned about this through working with a psychiatrist who suggested that he 'wanted to take a risk' and be honest about how 'they weren't helping'. This principle of 'positive risk taking', was not identified within the literature; yet was mentioned by four participants (P1, P2, P5 and P7) and it is an important finding of the study and an area for further research.

We conclude that there is still a role for compulsory treatment including use of coercive pressure in the treatment of patients presenting with eating disorders, including SEED. However, this needs to be done in a responsive and flexible way. The uncertainties of prognosis and outcomes as well as uncertainties of short- and long-term harms of coercion mean that we should avoid the equal and opposite errors of either aggressively pursuing recovery at all costs with diminishing returns and increasing suffering or abandoning patients and families as untreatable. Therefore, even when there is increased focus on managing symptoms or utilising palliative care, clinicians should always communicate that "the door is always open" and patients should be able to request to return to having active treatment as and when they feel ready.

'It's really important not to make decisions based on fear, so I try to find the courage to make decisions that I think are in someone's best interest, even if it does leave me feeling rather anxious about what other people might think and what will be said if things go wrong' [1].

Acknowledgments and thanks

The authors would like to thank Alex Ruck Keene KC for providing information about the recent Court of Protection cases concerning severe and enduring eating disorders. They would also like to thank Miss Sydney White for her kind discussion of the legal aspects of the Court of Protection cases which helped greatly in clarifying their understanding.

Finally, the authors would like to thank all the research participants in Jess Griffiths' Master's thesis research, whose anonymized quotes appear in this chapter. They would also like to thank all the courageous patients with SEED and their families, whose views and experiences have contributed over many years to shaping the thoughts and views of the authors and underpin the writing of this chapter.

Any errors in the chapter are the authors' alone.

Conflict of interest

The authors declare no conflict of interest.

Nomenclature

AN	anorexia nervosa
BN	bulimia nervosa
CBT	cognitive behavioural therapy
CoP	Court of Protection
CMHT	Community Mental Health Team
LSED	longstanding eating disorders
MHA	Mental Health Act 1983 and 2007. This is the mental health legislation of England and Wales which enables treatment of patients with mental disorders without their consent where there is risk to health or life and availability of treatment which is likely to be effective
NG	nasogastric tubes, passed through the nose down to the stomach to facilitate feeding
NHS	National Health Service, the government-funded healthcare service of United Kingdom
NICE	The National Institute for Health and Care Excellence
QoL	quality of life
SE-AN	severe and enduring anorexia nervosa
SEED	severe and enduring eating disorders
SEMI	severe and enduring mental disorders
SPICT	The Supportive & Palliative Care Indicators Tool

Author details

Adaeze Bradshaw[1], Jess Griffiths[2], Paul Robinson[3] and Jacinta Tan[4*]

1 Lincolnshire Partnership Foundation NHS Trust, Lincolnshire, United Kingdom

2 South London and Maudsley NHS Foundation Trust, London, United Kingdom

3 University College London, London, United Kingdom

4 Imperial College London, London, United Kingdom

*Address all correspondence to: jacinta.tan@imperial.ac.uk

References

[1] Griffiths J. What Are UK Clinicians' Perspectives on Working with Longstanding Anorexia Nervosa in Adult Patients after Experiencing a Patient Death? [Masters thesis]. Bath Spa University; 2025 (In print)

[2] Borson S, Katon W. Chronic anorexia nervosa: Medical mimic. The Western Journal of Medicine. 1981;**135**(4):257-265

[3] Strober M. Managing the chronic, treatment-resistant patient with anorexia nervosa. The International Journal of Eating Disorders. 2004;**36**(3):245-255

[4] Yager J. Chapter 16: Management of patients with chronic, intractable eating disorders. In: Yager J, Powers PS, editors. Clinical Manual of Eating Disorders. American Psychiatric Pub; 20 May 2008. pp. 407-440, 482

[5] Robinson P. Severe and Enduring Eating Disorder (SEED): Management of Complex Presentations of Anorexia and Bulimia Nervosa. John Wiley & Sons; 20 Apr 2009. p. 184

[6] Stuart SR, Tansey L, Quayle E. What we talk about when we talk about recovery: A systematic review and best-fit framework synthesis of qualitative literature. Journal of Mental Health (Abingdon, England). 2017;**26**(3):291-304

[7] Slade M. Mental illness and well-being: The central importance of positive psychology and recovery approaches. BMC Health Services Research. 2010;**10**(1):26

[8] Raykos BC, Erceg-Hurn DM, McEvoy PM, Fursland A, Waller G. Severe and enduring anorexia nervosa? Illness severity and duration are unrelated to outcomes from cognitive behaviour therapy. Journal of Consulting and Clinical Psychology. 2018;**86**(8):702-709

[9] Downs J, Ayton A, Collins L, Baker S, Missen H, Ibrahim A. Untreatable or unable to treat? Creating more effective and accessible treatment for long-standing and severe eating disorders. Lancet Psychiatry. 2023;**10**(2):146-154

[10] Wildes JE. Moving from "I know it when I see it" to an empirical classification of severe and enduring anorexia nervosa: Commentary on Wonderlich et al. (2020). The International Journal of Eating Disorders. 2020;**53**(8):1315-1317

[11] Wildes JE, Forbush KT, Hagan KE, Marcus MD, Attia E, Gianini LM, et al. Characterizing severe and enduring anorexia nervosa: An empirical approach. The International Journal of Eating Disorders. 2017;**50**(4):389-397

[12] Bamford B, Barras C, Sly R, Stiles-Shields C, Touyz S, Le Grange D, et al. Eating disorder symptoms and quality of life: Where should clinicians place their focus in severe and enduring anorexia nervosa? The International Journal of Eating Disorders. 2015;**48**(1):133-138

[13] Steinhausen HC. The outcome of anorexia nervosa in the 20th century. The American Journal of Psychiatry. 2002;**159**(8):1284-1293

[14] Robinson PH, Guidetti G, Kasriel J, Khawandanah J, Hughes M, Hachem Z. Can people with longstanding bulimia nervosa suffer from severe and enduring eating disorder? A qualitative

study. Journal of Eating Disorders. 2024;**12**(1):204

[15] Kiely L, Conti J, Hay P. Conceptualisation of severe and enduring anorexia nervosa: A qualitative meta-synthesis. BMC Psychiatry. 2023;**23**(1):1-26

[16] Treasure J, Russell G. The case for early intervention in anorexia nervosa: Theoretical exploration of maintaining factors. The British Journal of Psychiatry: The Journal of Mental Science. 2011;**199**(1):5-7

[17] Touyz S, Le Grange D, Lacey H, Hay P, Smith R, Maguire S, et al. Treating severe and enduring anorexia nervosa: A randomized controlled trial. Psychological Medicine. 2013;**43**(12):2501-2511

[18] Hergenroeder AC, Wiemann CM, Henges C, Dave A. Outcome of adolescents with eating disorders from an adolescent medicine service at a large children's hospital. International Journal of Adolescent Medicine and Health. 2015;**27**(1):49-56

[19] Nielsen S, Anckarsäter H, Gillberg C, Gillberg C, Råstam M, Wentz E. Effects of autism spectrum disorders on outcome in teenage-onset anorexia nervosa evaluated by the Morgan-Russell outcome assessment schedule: A controlled community-based study. Molecular Autism. 2015;**6**:14

[20] Fichter MM, Quadflieg N, Crosby RD, Koch S. Long-term outcome of anorexia nervosa: Results from a large clinical longitudinal study. The International Journal of Eating Disorders. 2017;**50**(9):1018-1030

[21] Herpertz-Dahlmann B, Dempfle A, Egberts KM, Kappel V, Konrad K, Vloet JA, et al. Outcome of childhood anorexia nervosa—The results of a five- to ten-year follow-up study. The International Journal of Eating Disorders. 2018;**51**(4):295-304

[22] Jagielska G, Kacperska I. Outcome, comorbidity and prognosis in anorexia nervosa. Psychiatria Polska. 2017;**51**(2):205-218

[23] Roff C, Cook-Cottone C. Assisted death in eating disorders: A systematic review of cases and clinical rationales. Frontiers in Psychiatry. 2024;**15**:1431771

[24] National Library of Medicine. Table 4, Levels of Evidence and Grading of Recommendations - Short- and Long-Term Use of Benzodiazepines in Patients with Generalized Anxiety Disorder: A Review of Guidelines [Internet]. Ottawa (ON), Bethesda, MD, USA: Canadian Agency for Drugs and Technologies in Health; National Center for Biothechnology Information, National Library of Medicine; 28 Jul 2014. Available from: https://www.ncbi.nlm.nih.gov/books/NBK254098/table/T4/#

[25] Himmerich H, Keeler JL, Tchanturia K, Treasure J. Treatment escalation for people with anorexia nervosa: Setting, therapies and nutritional interventions. Current Opinion in Psychiatry. 2024;**37**(6):404-416

[26] Fuller SJ, Chapman S, Cave E, Druce-Perkins J, Daniels P, Tan J. Nasogastric tube feeding under physical restraint on paediatric wards: Ethical, legal and practical considerations regarding this lifesaving intervention. BJPsych Bulletin. 2023;**47**(2):105-110

[27] Cave E, Tan J. Severe and enduring Anorexia Nervosa in the England and Wales Court of protection. International Journal of Mental Health and Capacity

Law. 2017;**23**(17):4-24. DOI: 10.19164/ijmhcl.v2017i23.629

[28] Dyer C. Anorexic woman cannot be force fed, judge rules. BMJ. 2012;**345**:e5804. DOI: 10.1136/bmj.e5804

[29] Ramsay R, Ward A, Treasure J, Russell GFM. Compulsory treatment in anorexia nervosa: Short-term benefits and long-term mortality. The British Journal of Psychiatry. 1999;**175**(2):147-153

[30] Elzakkers IFFM, Danner UN, Hoek HW, Schmidt U, Van Elburg AA. Compulsory treatment in anorexia nervosa: A review. The International Journal of Eating Disorders. 2014;**47**(8):845-852

[31] Zohar-Beja A. Compulsory Treatment for Anorexia Nervosa in Israel Clinical Outcomes and Compliance: A Retrospective Cohort Study. [Masters thesis]. Haifa, Israel: University of Haifa; 2013. Available from: https://www.proquest.com/openview/ac67e010b62335ee1f1022efd04a62b5/1?pq-origsite=gscholar&cbl=2026366&diss=y [Accessed: June 17 June, 2025]

[32] Garner DM, Garfinkel PE, Bemis KM. A multidimensional psychotherapy for anorexia nervosa. The International Journal of Eating Disorders. 1982;**1**(2):3-46

[33] Mental Health Act 1983. Available from: https://www.legislation.gov.uk/ukpga/1983/20/contents

[34] Túry F, Szalai T, Szumska I. Compulsory treatment in eating disorders: Control, provocation, and the coercion paradox. Journal of Clinical Psychology. 2019;**75**(8):1444-1454

[35] Goldner E. Treatment refusal in anorexia nervosa. The International Journal of Eating Disorders. 1989;**8**(3):297-306

[36] Beauchamp TL. Principles of Biomedical Ethics. Vol. 20. Oxford, England: Oxford University Press; 1989

[37] Herring B, Paraskeva N, Tollow P, Harcourt D. Women's initial experiences of their appearance after mastectomy and/or breast reconstruction: A qualitative study. Psycho-Oncology. 2019;**28**(10):2076-2082

[38] Mental Capacity Act 2005. Available from: https://www.legislation.gov.uk/ukpga/2005/9

[39] Jamieson SK, Tan J, Piekunka K, Calvert S, Anderson S. Navigating the ethical complexities of severe and enduring (longstanding) eating disorders: Tools for critically reflective practice and collaborative decision-making. Journal of Eating Disorders. 2024;**12**(1):134

[40] RK AA Mental Capacity Law and Policy. Anorexia, the Court of Protection and the changing calculus of decision-making. 2025. Available from: https://www.mentalcapacitylawandpolicy.org.uk/anorexia-the-court-of-protection-and-the-changing-calculus-of-decision-making/

[41] Schreyer CC, Coughlin JW, Makhzoumi SH, Redgrave GW, Hansen JL, Guarda AS. Perceived coercion in inpatients with anorexia nervosa: Associations with illness severity and hospital course. The International Journal of Eating Disorders. 2016;**49**(4):407-412

[42] Guarda AS, Pinto AM, Coughlin JW, Hussain S, Haug NA, Heinberg LJ. Perceived coercion and change in perceived need for admission in patients hospitalized for eating

disorders. The American Journal of Psychiatry. 2007;**164**(1):108-114

[43] Tan J, Hope T, Stewart A. Competence to refuse treatment in anorexia nervosa. International Journal of Law and Psychiatry. 2003;**26**(6):697-707

[44] Tan J, Stewart A, Fitzpatrick R, Hope RA. Competence to make treatment decisions in anorexia nervosa: Thinking processes and values. Philosophy, Psychiatry, and Psychology. 2006;**13**(4):267-282

[45] Tan JOA, Hope T, Stewart A. Anorexia nervosa and personal identity: The accounts of patients and their parents. International Journal of Law and Psychiatry. 2003;**26**(5):533-548

[46] Fuller S, Sheridan E, Tan J, Nicholls D. 'We are not trained to do clinical work': Security staff providing physical restraint for NGT feeding in English paediatric wards-a qualitative multi-informant study. BMJ Open. 2024;**14**(12):e085955

[47] Falcoski P, Philpot U, Tan J, Hudson LD, Fuller SJ. Nasogastric tube feeding in line with new dietetic guidelines for the treatment of anorexia nervosa in a specialist children and adolescent inpatient unit: A case series. Journal of Human Nutrition and Dietetics: Official Journal of the British Dietetic Association. 2021;**34**(1):33-41

[48] Tan JOA, Hope T, Stewart A, Fitzpatrick R. Control and compulsory treatment in anorexia nervosa: The views of patients and parents. International Journal of Law and Psychiatry. 2003;**26**(6):627-645

[49] Hope T, Tan J, Stewart A, McMillan J. Agency, ambivalence and authenticity: The many ways in which anorexia nervosa can affect autonomy. International Journal of Law in Context. 2013;**9**(1):20-36

[50] Diedrichs PC. Sociocultural environment and internalization of the thin ideal as eating disorder risk factors. In: Wade T, editor. Encyclopedia of Feeding and Eating Disorders. Singapore: Springer; 2015. pp. 1-5. DOI: 10.1007/978-981-287-087-2_89-1

[51] Stanghellini G, Castellini G, Brogna P, Faravelli C, Ricca V. Identity and eating disorders (IDEA): A questionnaire evaluating identity and embodiment in eating disorder patients. Psychopathology. 2012;**45**(3):147-158

[52] Lekeka M. Breast Cancer treatment (mastectomy experiences) may initiate individuation process that redefines identities: A systematic review. Alternation: Interdisciplinary Journal for the Study of the Arts and Humanities in Southern Africa. 3 Jan 2023;**41**(sed):517-545

[53] Faria BM, Rodrigues IM, Marquez LV, da Silva Pires U, de Oliveira SV. The impact of mastectomy on body image and sexuality in women with breast cancer: A systematic review. Psicooncología. 2021;**18**(1):91-115

[54] Curie M. What is End of Life Care? Support in the Last Year of Life. Available from: https://www.mariecurie.org.uk/information/getting-care/end-of-life-care

[55] Overview | End of Life Care for Adults: Service Delivery | Guidance | NICE. Available from: https://www.nice.org.uk/guidance/ng142

[56] What End of Life Care Involves - NHS. Available from: https://www.nhs.uk/conditions/end-of-life-care/what-it-involves-and-when-it-starts/

[57] Coping with a Terminal Illness - NHS. Available from: https://www.nhs.uk/conditions/end-of-life-care/your-wellbeing/coping-with-a-terminal-illness/

[58] Orlovic M, Droney J, Vickerstaff V, Rosling J, Bearne A, Powell M, et al. Accuracy of clinical predictions of prognosis at the end-of-life: Evidence from routinely collected data in urgent care records. BMC Palliative Care. 2023;**22**(1):51

[59] Treasure J, Stein D, Maguire S. Has the time come for a staging model to map the course of eating disorders from high risk to severe enduring illness? An examination of the evidence. Early Intervention in Psychiatry. 2015;**9**(3):173-184

[60] Xue H, Chen Y, Zhou Y. Radioimmunotherapy: A game-changer for advanced non-small cell lung cancer. Frontiers in Immunology. 2024;**15**:1522508

[61] Utkarsh K, Srivastava N, Kumar S, Khan A, Dagar G, Kumar M, et al. CAR-T cell therapy: A game-changer in cancer treatment and beyond. Clinical and Translational Oncology: Official Publication of the Federation of Spanish Oncology Societies and of the National Cancer Institute of Mexico. 2024;**26**(6):1300-1318

[62] Long MW, Ward ZJ, Wright DR, Rodriguez P, Tefft NW, Austin SB. Cost-effectiveness of 5 public health approaches to prevent eating disorders. American Journal of Preventive Medicine. 2022;**63**(6):935-943

[63] Rohrbach PJ, Dingemans AE, van Furth EF, Spinhoven P, van Ginkel JR, Bauer S, et al. Cost-effectiveness of three internet-based interventions for eating disorders: A randomized controlled trial. The International Journal of Eating Disorders. 2022;**55**(8):1143-1155

[64] Koreshe E, Paxton S, Miskovic-Wheatley J, Bryant E, Le A, Maloney D, et al. Prevention and early intervention in eating disorders: Findings from a rapid review. Journal of Eating Disorders. 2023;**11**(1):38

[65] Birch E, Downs J, Ayton A. Harm reduction in severe and long-standing anorexia nervosa: Part of the journey but not the destination-a narrative review with lived experience. Journal of Eating Disorders. 2024;**12**(1):140

[66] Gaudiani JL, Bogetz A, Yager J. Terminal anorexia nervosa: Three cases and proposed clinical characteristics. Journal of Eating Disorders. 2022;**10**(1):23

[67] Phillipou A. The importance of terminology, lived experience inclusion and scientific discussion regarding end-of-life care in anorexia nervosa: A response to Gaudiani et al. Journal of Eating Disorders. 2023;**11**(1):1-4. DOI: 10.1186/s40337-023-00872-2

[68] Elwyn R. A lived experience response to the proposed diagnosis of terminal anorexia nervosa: Learning from iatrogenic harm, ambivalence and enduring hope. Journal of Eating Disorders. 2023;**11**(1):1-18. DOI: 10.1186/s40337-022-00729-0

[69] Westmoreland P, Parks L, Lohse K, Mehler P. Severe and enduring anorexia nervosa and futility: A time for every purpose? The Psychiatric Clinics of North America. 2021;**44**(4):603-611

[70] World Health Organization. Palliative Care. Cuid Paliat. Available from: https://iris.who.int/handle/10665/44024

[71] Curie M. What is Palliative Care? Available from: https://www.mariecurie.org.uk/information/getting-care/palliative-care

[72] www.rcpsych.ac.uk RCPsych Issues Statement on Eating Disorder Patients Being Offered Palliative Care. Available from: https://www.rcpsych.ac.uk/news-and-features/latest-news/detail/2023/05/17/rcpsych-issues-statement-on-eating-disorder-patients-being-offered-palliative-care

[73] Gardini V, Tomei G, Tomba E. Iatrogenic factors in the treatment of Anorexia Nervosa. La Clinica Terapeutica (supplemento). 2022:30-30

[74] Russell J, Mulvey B, Bennett H, Donnelly B, Frig E. Harm minimization in severe and enduring anorexia nervosa. International Review of Psychiatry. 2019;**31**(4):391-402

[75] Varkey B. Principles of clinical ethics and their application to practice. Medical Principles and Practice. 2021;**30**(1):17-28

[76] Tan JOA, Gray F. Primary care in eating disorders. In: RobinsonP, WadeT, Herpertz-DahlmannB, Fernandez-Aranda F, Treasure J, Wonderlich S, editors. Eating Disorders: An International Comprehensive View. Cham: Springer International Publishing; 2023. pp. 1-25. DOI: 10.1007/978-3-030-97416-9_53-1

[77] Highet G, Crawford D, Murray SA, Boyd K. Development and evaluation of the supportive and palliative care indicators tool (SPICT): A mixed-methods study. BMJ Supportive & Palliative Care. 2014;**4**(3):285-290

[78] Koffman J, Yorganci E, Yi D, Gao W, Murtagh F, Pickles A, et al. Managing uncertain recovery for patients nearing the end of life in hospital: A mixed-methods feasibility cluster randomised controlled trial of the AMBER care bundle. Trials. 2019;**20**(1):506

Chapter 2

Digital Transformation of Eating Disorder Care in Chile: "Espacio Balance", a Case Study of Innovation in an Unequal Health System

Melina Vogel and Aurora Gil

Abstract

The COVID-19 pandemic exacerbated existing barriers to mental health treatment, particularly for individuals with eating disorders (EDs) in countries with the limited access to specialised care. In Chile, where public and private healthcare systems face structural and geographic constraints, the need for accessible and scalable interventions became critical. This chapter presents Espacio Balance (EB), an innovative virtual programme developed by the Eating Disorders Unit (Unidad de Trastornos alimentarios, UTAL) at the Red de Salud UC Christus, Chile, in response to these challenges. EB was designed to deliver multidisciplinary, evidence-based group interventions online for patients with EDs and their caregivers. EB integrates therapeutic workshops tailored to patients' recovery phases and clinical profiles. A distinctive feature is the Online Meal Support Group (OMSG), which facilitates supervised shared meals, particularly benefiting patients in remote areas. Quantitative data from 54 female patients with anorexia nervosa demonstrated the statistically significant improvements in body mass index (BMI) over a 90-day period. An exploratory qualitative study is currently underway to assess patients perceptions of the virtual sessions. Preliminary findings suggest enhanced emotional support, normalisation of eating behaviours and reduced isolation through virtual group participation. In summary, the programme fosters continuity of care, family engagement and professional collaboration, despite technological and motivational challenges. Now in its fifth year, EB continues to evolve through hybrid formats and peer-led support initiatives. It represents a cost-effective and impactful model for addressing ED treatment gaps in under-resourced contexts. This chapter underscores the potential of virtual interventions to transform access, quality and continuity of care for EDs and highlights the importance of community, adaptability and systemic collaboration in the digital delivery of mental health services.

Keywords: eating disorders, online treatment, telemedicine, virtual group therapy, equity in healthcare, digital innovation

1. Introduction

The provision of support programmes for families and patients is of fundamental importance in the treatment of eating disorders (EDs) [1–3], particularly in societies where mental health services are underfunded and access to treatments provided by specialised teams is limited and costly. Empirical evidence has identified emotional and practical support from primary care health professionals and family members as crucial factors in the initiation of treatment [4]. In less developed countries, the absence of specialised EDs teams in large cities has been identified as a significant geographical barrier to access [4]. This has been shown to result in considerable travel distances for patients and their families, which represents a significant barrier to treatment access. Moreover, the absence of specialists may result in inappropriate treatment for patients seeking help from their healthcare system. The failure to recognise an eating disorder or the provision of inappropriate recommendations has been identified as important barriers to successful treatment [5].

2. The Chilean context: General mental health and eating disorder (ED) care and the impact of the COVID-19 pandemic

This issue assumes particular pertinence in a country characterised by geographical challenges, such as Chile, which extends over a span of more than 4000 kilometres. Despite the high demand for eating disorders treatments and the fact that intensive programmes, such as day hospitals, have been widely accepted worldwide for the past two decades, Chile currently has only a limited number of centres that offer such interventions. The nation's geographical characteristics, including its extensive and isolated topography, have been identified as significant factors contributing to the challenges in accessing healthcare resources and human capital for mental healthcare [6]. The Chilean health care financing system is a mixed public and private model, with inequalities in the coverage of psychiatric and psychological interventions, whether delivered in ambulatory, residential, in-person or virtual environments. The financial burden of these challenges is substantial, with families often assuming significant out-of-pocket expenses for mental healthcare services. The implementation of mental health policies in Chile has been confronted with a number of structural, cultural and managerial difficulties. The scarcity of financial and human resources is a salient issue. The budget is also limited. Historically, mental health has received a low proportion of the total health budget (approximately 2–3%, far from the 5% recommended by the WHO) [7]. Both the private and public systems are overburdened: the combination of high demand and a shortage of staff results in extensive waiting lists for mental healthcare services.

3. Telemedicine interventions as diagnostic, treatment and support tools

During the period of national lockdown that ensued in response to the pandemic, the utilisation of online platforms witnessed a marked increase in its importance [8]. The repercussions of the COVID-19 pandemic on mental health, as emphasised by the United Nations in June 2022, have been substantial, with a 25–27% escalation in the prevalence of anxiety and depression in the general population during the initial year of the pandemic [9]. A similar trend was observed in the case of eating disorders, which also worsened during the health crisis [10]. This phenomenon was also observed by our team, with a 30% surge in consultations, with a notable 70% of these cases involving patients under the age of 25 [11]. The restrictions imposed by the pandemic compelled us to explore alternative telemedicine approaches to address the augmented demand for care related to these issues.

Telemedicine-based interventions have emerged as a powerful tool for diagnosis and treatment, as well as an effective way to provide help, emotional containment and support, and are gradually becoming part of the treatment of various mental health problems, including ED, given the benefits of their use, which include cost reduction and the ability to provide patients with broader access to mental health care [12–15].

One of the key aspects of ED treatment is the social component, which has been shown to be crucial in the onset and maintenance of symptoms, as well as in treatment seeking and maintenance [16, 17]. The integration of social support elements into treatment programmes has shown promising results, suggesting that it may be useful in achieving longer-term positive treatment outcomes [18]. Group dynamics significantly influence the effectiveness of eating disorder treatments. Research indicates that positive group interactions can enhance recovery, while negative dynamics may hinder progress. Group dynamics have been shown to have a significant impact on patients and their families, fostering a sense of connection and empathy [19]. When general mental health content and specific ED-focused materials are taught, this connection is easier to achieve.

4. The UC health network and UTAL (eating disorder unit): The implementation of Espacio Balance

The Pontificia Universidad Católica de Chile (PUC) is widely regarded as one of the most prestigious universities in Latin America. It is associated with the most extensive private health network in Chile (Red de Salud UC Christus), with the capacity to provide full continuity of treatment to its patients, in a wide range of clinical presentations and levels of complexity. The UC Health Network has a specialised Eating Disorders team consisting of psychiatrists, paediatricians, internists, nutritionists, psychologists, occupational therapists and nurses for the management of patients aged 15 years and older (Eating Disorders Unit, UTAL). The UTAL operates in various outpatient centres, day treatment, inpatient units and through telemedicine. The majority of patients admitted to the UTAL are treated as outpatients and are referred from various locations throughout the country. During the strictest phase of the COVID-19 lockdown, the UTAL initiated an online programme, Espacio Balance (EB), which took advantage of the emerging use of digital technologies to improve access to therapeutic interventions, complementing the ongoing efforts of the clinical team. Espacio Balance was conceptualised as a matrix of virtual group workshops whose main objectives were, on the one hand, to reduce the sense of isolation for both patients and their families, and on the other hand, to offer specific interventions for the treatment of eating disorders, taking into account the diversity in their clinical presentations, the ages of the participants and their stage of recovery.

5. Characteristics of Espacio Balance (EB)

EB has rapidly established itself as a central and innovative component in the treatment of EDs in Chile. Its model provides essential support not only for individuals affected by EDs but also for their families, highlighting the importance of systemically informed interventions.

The therapeutic activities offered by EB are diverse and multidisciplinary, with workshops facilitated by specialists in psychology, psychiatry, nutrition, occupational therapy and physical rehabilitation. These workshops are carefully tailored to each participant's treatment phase, clinical diagnosis and developmental stage. Their content addresses key domains of recovery including self-esteem, body image, social and emotional regulation, and relapse prevention. This individualised therapeutic experience reflects a biopsychosocial model of care.

All interventions are grounded in evidence-based frameworks, including Cognitive Behavioural Therapy (CBT), Dialectical Behaviour Therapy (DBT), Mindfulness, Mindful Eating and occupational therapy-based tools. Strategies aimed at restructuring dysfunctional cognitions related to food and the body, resolving interpersonal conflicts, and reintegrating physical activity and occupational identity (OMSP) are systematically incorporated. These integrative approaches contribute to a holistic recovery process that aligns with the international standards of care [20, 21].

A hallmark innovation of EB is its Online Meal Support Group (OMSG) – a virtual shared space where patients eat together under professional supervision. This initiative supports the refeeding process and encourages the normalisation of eating behaviours within the home setting. Recent studies on hybrid interventions [22, 23] provide some evidence that such online approaches can extend specialised support to geographically remote or underserved areas. These online group settings not only promote nutritional recovery but also foster a sense of peer support and mitigate isolation – outcomes highlighted as critical for adherence and resilience [24, 25].

All EB activities are delivered *via* the Zoom platform. Patients receive personalised workshop schedules, collaboratively designed by the clinical team, the patient and their family, to match their treatment phase, diagnosis and specific needs. Group sessions – lasting 60 minutes – are held for adolescents, adults and carers, with groups comprising up to 20 participants. Each session is facilitated by one or two clinicians, ensuring both clinical containment and therapeutic efficacy. The group format, shown to enhance both emotional connection and therapeutic engagement, is central to EB's design [26].

Participation in EB is governed by principles of confidentiality, respect and mutual collaboration. These expectations are communicated through a formal commitment letter signed by both the patient and their family prior to enrolment. This step reflects a growing emphasis on collaborative care models that include family systems as active participants in recovery [27, 28].

In alignment with this systemic approach, caregivers are also encouraged to participate in EB's group sessions, including those based on the Maudsley Method. Furthermore, they are invited to observe and support the Online Meal Support Groups, providing them with both insight and practical tools to assist their loved ones. Evidence indicates that such family based online interventions may reduce caregiver distress and strengthen family functioning [24, 29].

Through its integrative, evidence-informed and family-cantered model, Espacio Balance stands as an exemplar of how virtual group-based interventions can effectively expand access to treatment, enhance clinical outcomes and foster a supportive therapeutic community.

6. Impact: Reception of the programme by families and teams

Within months of its implementation, EB was well accepted by both patients and the team, mainly because it removed some of the primary barriers to access to treatment in 2020. However, the platform continued beyond the pandemic and evolved into a stable operational model. It was soon apparent that the incorporation of EB had a significant impact on patients, families, therapists and the UTAL as a network, according to the information shared in clinical meetings and individual sessions with patients. For patients and families, the platform appeared to offer the benefits of in-person experiences, providing a secure environment in which to meet others facing similar challenges and to share experiences and knowledge through treatment stages. The exchange of health concerns appeared to facilitate the establishment of a sense of community among individuals affected by ED and their families, thereby providing a platform for mutual support and companionship. The primary issues that were addressed included the paucity of information about ED, the prevalence of myths, stigmatisation, social isolation, difficulties in resuming eating and maintaining motivation for recovery. For therapists, clinical action was enriched with a sense of efficacy, teamwork and purpose. In the context of the UTAL, EB facilitated effective continuity of care across all levels of complexity, thereby enabling patients receiving day treatment or inpatient care to transition to outpatient care without losing contact with this new support network.

In 2023, we aimed to evaluate the positive impact of the Online Meal Support Group (OMSG) at Espacio Balance (EB) as part of a blended virtual and in-person treatment approach for EDs [30]. A retrospective review was conducted on 54 female patients diagnosed with AN, with a mean age of 18.4 years (SD ± 2.6). Their mean BMI at the time of entry into the OMSG was 17.6 kg/m^2 (SD ± 1.3). Paired sample *t*-tests showed statistically significant weight gains at each follow-up point, increasing their mean BMI to 18.5 kg/m^2 at 45 days and 19.2 kg/m^2 at 90 days (**Table 1**).

We hypothesised that patients participating in OMSG, adequately guided by trained therapists, began to function as a supportive virtual community. In the course of individual therapy, a significant number of patients reported that they had not previously encountered interventions of this nature. Rather, they had been influenced by social media promoting restrictive diets, extreme thinness or bodybuilding. Many of these patients held the belief that social acceptance could only be achieved by adhering to rigid aesthetic standards and unhealthy eating behaviours. This perception is widely acknowledged by other experts in the field of eating disorders, as reflected in the review by Dane and Bathia [31]. The OMSG appeared to have the potential to correct those misconceptions and exert an influence on young individuals by offering an alternative community experience that emphasised the normalisation of eating

Comparison	Mean difference (SD)	95% CI (lower/upper)	*t*	*df*	*p*-value	Effect size (Cohen's *d*)
Entry vs. 45 days	2.52 (2.37)	1.87/3.17	7.81	53	<0.001	−1.064
45 Days vs. 90 days	1.88 (1.66)	1.43/2.33	8.31	53	<0.001	−1.131
Entry vs. 90 days	4.41 (2.82)	3.63/5.17	11.48	53	<0.001	−1.563

Table 1.
Paired sample t*-test results for weight progression in EB.*

behaviours and amplified messages of health and self-care. A notable limitation of this study was the absence of a control group, which was due to the ethical challenges involved in withholding an intervention that appeared both urgent and necessary.

An exploratory qualitative study is currently being conducted to ascertain patients' perceptions of the interventions implemented within the virtual meal setting, with a particular emphasis on the normalisation of eating behaviours [32]. The study will describe the benefits and barriers of virtual meal sessions, the interventions of therapists and peer interventions. This study specifically targets patients diagnosed with AN and atypical AN who have consistently participated in the virtual meal programme for a minimum of 3 months and are over the age of 18. The descriptive analysis of the interviews has led to the identification of key themes regarding the patients' perceptions of the virtual meal environment, and preliminary results can be organised around the following concepts:

- Initial experience: Patients enter the virtual meal sessions with a mixture of emotions, including uncertainty, anger, shyness, fear of judgement, insecurity and, in some cases, a sense of exclusion. The initial experience is marked by challenges such as adjusting to a different environment from their home and the perceived obligation to participate.

- Perceived changes: As patients become more involved with the virtual meal group, they start to see it as a pleasant and beneficial space. They value the opportunity to help and be helped, to feel reflected in the experiences of others and to experience a sense of group belonging.

- Modification of eating symptoms: The virtual meal sessions appear to facilitate significant changes in patients' relationships with food. These include the redefinition of difficult foods, a reduction in guilt and anxiety surrounding eating, the incorporation of challenging foods into daily life and the development of a more intuitive approach to eating.

- Emotional and family experience changes: The virtual meal programme impacts eating behaviours, as well as emotional experiences and perceptions of illness at the family level.

- Factors contributing to change: It is important to note that the observed changes can be attributed to a number of factors. These include the time that has elapsed since the commencement of treatment, the specific interventions that have been implemented during the virtual meal sessions and the contributions made by the patients themselves. Patients value the opportunity to hear others' experiences, feel represented, reduce feelings of isolation and both give and receive support.

7. Implementing and managing EB

7.1 Internal coordination

A central factor contributing to the success of EB is its strong and efficient internal coordination, which stands as a defining feature of the programme. The multidisciplinary team UTAL, collaborates closely to develop and implement integrated treatment plans tailored to each patient's individual needs. The programme's effectiveness is further strengthened by continuous intra-team communication, which allows for timely adjustments to therapeutic strategies in response to the patient's evolving progress and clinical challenges.

The collaboration between various professionals is central to the success of EB. Psychiatrists monitor mental health symptoms, while dietitians focus on nutritional rehabilitation, and psychologists implement behavioural interventions. This multidisciplinary collaboration ensures that patients receive well-rounded care that addresses both the psychological and physical aspects of their eating disorder. Regular team meetings help keep everyone aligned on patient progress and necessary adjustments. EB's clinical coordination involves constant communication between the UTAL team and the virtual platform coordinators to ensure smooth operations. Scheduling of sessions, availability of the right professionals for each session and real-time support are all critical to the programme's success. Technological support also plays a pivotal role in ensuring the functionality of the virtual platform. The coordination of both clinical and logistical components ensures that patients' needs are met without interruption. Family involvement is a keystone of EB's therapeutic model. Group sessions, based on the Maudsley Method, are designed to help caregivers develop effective coping strategies to support their loved ones. These sessions foster a collaborative care environment and empower families to take an active role in the recovery process.

Despite its successes, EB has encountered several implementation challenges. Some difficulties included technological barriers, such as limited internet connectivity and low digital literacy, especially among patients in rural areas. To mitigate these issues, the team conducted virtual orientation sessions and distributed support materials to enhance access and usability. Another challenge was patients' initial discomfort with the virtual format, which some feared that it would be impersonal or less effective than in-person therapy. To overcome this, the team introduced icebreakers and interactive sessions, fostering a more welcoming and engaging environment. Over time, patients saw the benefits of virtual group interactions, and family members were encouraged to foster supportive home environments, extending the sense of community beyond the virtual sessions.

Maintaining long-term engagement in a virtual setting is challenging, particularly as the lack of in-person contact may lead to a sense of detachment or loss of accountability. Some patients also experienced burnout or frustration with the repetitive nature of virtual therapy. The team adopted a flexible structure that continuously adapts to keep patients engaged. The programme's content is regularly updated to remain relevant and interesting, and patient feedback is regularly solicited to ensure the programme stays dynamic and centred on the patient's needs. Lastly, as the pandemic subsided, some patients and families expressed a preference for returning to in-person therapy. The team highlighted the unique benefits of virtual therapy, such as accessibility for remote patients, flexible scheduling and a supportive environment, and used patient feedback to refine the programme and reinforce its effectiveness.

8. Key insights and future directions

As Espacio Balance celebrates its fifth year of operation, its impact on the treatment of EDs in Chile is undeniable. Moving forward, the programme aims to enhance its offerings and address emerging challenges.

Enhanced technological integration: The continued development of technological infrastructure is vital to EB's future success. Future plans include integrating more interactive features, such as real-time feedback and data analytics, to monitor patient progress and adjust treatments dynamically. Additionally, AI-powered tools are being explored to personalise patient care even further.

Increased family and peer support: Greater involvement of patients who have made significant progress can help cultivate a stronger sense of community within the programme. These individuals can serve as mentors, offering guidance and encouragement to others, which fosters a shared sense of purpose. Peer-led initiatives play a crucial role in strengthening this sense of belonging and providing motivation for others [24]. In this area, we are developing hybrid groups that combine in-person and virtual interactions, promoting face-to-face communication, autonomy and goal achievement. These groups are designed to help participants reach a point where they can transition out of *Espacio Balance* – essentially marking the completion of their treatment journey and a sense of "graduation".

Sustainability beyond the pandemic: EB has proven to be cost-effective, especially for patients in remote areas who might otherwise struggle to access traditional in person treatment. Continued investment in resources, both human and financial, is essential to ensuring EB's sustainability as a long-term solution for EDs treatment.

Author details

Melina Vogel[1,2*] and Aurora Gil[1]

1 Eating Disorders Unit of the UC Christus Health Network, Santiago, Chile

2 Faculty of Medicine, Psychiatry Department, Pontificia Universidad Católica de Chile, Santiago, Chile

*Address all correspondence to: mvogel@uc.cl

References

[1] Hannah L, Cross M, Baily H, Grimwade K, Clarke T, Allan SM. A systematic review of the impact of carer interventions on outcomes for patients with eating disorders. Eating and Weight Disorders. 2022;**27**:1953-1962

[2] Grennan L, Nicula M, Pellegrini D, Giuliani K, Crews E, Webb C, et al. "I'm not alone": A qualitative report of experiences among parents of children with eating disorders attending virtual parent-led peer support groups. Journal of Eating Disorders. 2022;**10**:195

[3] Monaghan M, Doyle L. 'It stopped you thinking about food'—The experiences of mealtimes and attending a post-meal support group for young people with anorexia nervosa. International Journal of Mental Health Nursing. 2023;**32**:128-138

[4] Reuter L, Kastner D, Schmidt J, Weigel A, Voderholzer U, Seidel M, et al. The development and psychometric evaluation of FABIANA-checklist: A scale to assess factors influencing treatment initiation in anorexia nervosa. Journal of Eating Disorders. 2021;**9**:144

[5] Castañeda F, Cerda J, Jara R, Riestra F, Urrejola P, Vogel M, et al. Exploration of barriers to treatment for patients with eating disorders in Chile. Journal of Eating Disorders. 2024;**12**(1):160

[6] de Medicina F, Católica PU, de Chile. Salud mental. En Salud para Chile: Reflexiones y aportes de Medicina UC a la discusión pública. 2nd ed. Pontificia Universidad Católica de Chile; 2024. pp. 106-125

[7] World Health Organization & Ministerio de Salud de Chile. Informe Sobre el Sistema de Salud Mental en Chile: Informe de la evaluación del Sistema de Salud Mental en Chile Usando World Health Organization - Assessment Instrument for Mental Health Systems (WHO-AIMS). Santiago de Chile: OMS y Ministerio de Salud; 2006. Available from: https://diprece.minsal.cl/wrdprss_minsal/wp-content/uploads/2016/02/Ministerio-de-Salud_2006_Informe-WHO-AIMS.pdf

[8] Taylor CB, Fitzsimmons-Craft EE, Graham AK. Digital technology can revolutionize mental health services delivery: The COVID-19 crisis as a catalyst for change. The International Journal of Eating Disorders. 2020;**53**:1155-1157

[9] World Health Organization. World Mental Health Report: transforming Mental Health for all. Geneva: World Health Organization; 2022. Licence: CC BY-NC-SA 3.0 IGO

[10] Devoe D, Han A, Anderson A, Katzman DK, Patten SB, Soumbasis A, et al. The impact of the COVID-19 pandemic on eating disorders: A systematic review. The International Journal of Eating Disorders. 2023;**56**(1):5-25

[11] Vogel M, Urrejola P, Irribarra V. Trastornos de la conducta alimentaria en adolescentes chilenos: una epidemia silenciosa. Temas de la Agenda Pública. 2021;**17**(159):1-12

[12] Hilty DM, Ferrer DC, Parish MB, Johnston B, Callahan EJ, Yellowlees PM. The effectiveness of telemental health: a 2013 review. Telemedicine Journal and E-Health. 2013;**19**(6):444-454

[13] Bashshur RL, Shannon GW, Bashshur N, Yellowlees PM. The

empirical evidence for telemedicine interventions in mental disorders. Telemedicine Journal and E-Health. 2016;**22**(2):87-113. DOI: 10.1089/tmj.2015.0206. Epub 2015 Dec 1

[14] Hagi K, Kurokawa S, Takamiya A, Fujikawa M, Kinoshita S, Iizuka M, et al. Telepsychiatry versus face-to-face treatment: systematic review and meta-analysis of randomised controlled trials. The British Journal of Psychiatry. 2023;**223**(3):407-414

[15] Sharma G, Devan K. The effectiveness of telepsychiatry: thematic review. BJPsych Bulletin. 2023;**47**(2):82-89. DOI: 10.1192/bjb.2021.115

[16] Leonidas C, Dos Santos MA. Social support networks and eating disorders: an integrative review of the literature. Neuropsychiatric Disease and Treatment. 2014;**10**:915-927

[17] Linville D, Brown T, Sturm K, T MD. Eating disorders and social support: perspectives of recovered individuals. Eating Disorders. 2012;**20**(3):216-231. DOI: 10.1080/10640266.2012.668480

[18] Ramjan LM, Smith BW, Miskovic-Wheatley J, Pathrose SP, Hay PJ. Social support for young people with eating disorders-an integrative review. International Journal of Mental Health Nursing. 2024;**33**(6):1615-1636

[19] Langley J, Treasure J, Todd G. Caring for a Loved One with an Eating Disorder: The New Maudsley Skills-Based Training Manual. 1st ed. NY: Routledge; 2019. pp. 3-13

[20] Fairburn C, (G.). Cooper. Cognitive behaviour therapy for eating disorders: A "transdiagnostic" theory and treatment. Behaviour Research and Therapy. 2003;**41**(5):509-528

[21] Hibbs R, Rhind C, Leppanen J, Treasure J. Interventions for caregivers of someone with an eating disorder: a meta-analysis. The International Journal of Eating Disorders. 2015;**48**(4):349-361

[22] Bryan D, Rowlands K, Macdonald P, Cardi V, Ambwani S, Arcelus J, et al. Transition support for patients admitted to intensive treatment for anorexia nervosa: Qualitative study of patient and carer experiences of a hybrid online guided self-help intervention (ECHOMAN-TRA). BJPsych Open. 2024;**10**:e81. DOI: 10.1192/bjo.2023.642

[23] Rohrbach PJ, Dingemans AE, Spinhoven P, Van Ginkel JR, Fokkema M, Wilderjans TF, et al. Effectiveness of an online self-help program, expert-patient support, and their combination for eating disorders: Results from a randomized controlled trial. The International Journal of Eating Disorders. 2022;**55**(10):1361-1373. DOI: 10.1002/eat.23785. Epub 2022 Jul 30

[24] Spencer L, Schmidt-Hantke J, Allen K, Gordon G, Potterton R, Musiat P, et al. A web-based intervention for carers of individuals with anorexia nervosa (we can): Trial protocol of a randomised controlled trial investigating the effectiveness of different levels of support. Internet Interventions. 2019;**16**:76-85. DOI: 10.1016/j.invent.2018.02.005

[25] Nicula M, Grennan L, Loewen T, Crews E, Giuliani K, Webb C, et al. Virtual parent-led peer support groups for parents of children with eating disorders: A mixed methods feasibility study. International Journal of Eating Disorders. 2023;**56**(11):2107-2119. DOI: 10.1002/eat.24042

[26] Murray MF, Kandel JS, Rifkin R, Hendelman J, Tsen J, Haedt-Matt AA. Initial examination of virtual

support groups as a resource for caregivers of individuals with eating disorders. Eating Disorders: The Journal of Treatment & Prevention. Advance online publication. 2025. DOI: 10.1080/10640266.2025.2489864

[27] Grover M, Naumann U, Mohammad-Dar L, Glennon D, Ringwood S, Eisler I, et al. A randomized controlled trial of an internet-based cognitive-behavioural skills package for carers of people with anorexia nervosa. Psychological Medicine. 2011;**41**(12):2581-2591. DOI: 10.1017/S0033291711000766. Epub 2011 May 20

[28] Treasure J, Schmidt U, Macdonald P. The Clinician's Guide to Collaborative Caring in Eating Disorders: The New Maudsley Method. London, UK: Routledge; 2009

[29] Katsuki F, Watanabe N, Kondo M, Sawada H, Yamada A. Remote family education and support program for parents of patients with adolescent and early adulthood eating disorders based on interpersonal psychotherapy: Study protocol for a pilot randomized controlled trial. Journal of Eating Disorders. 2024;**12**:61. DOI: 10.1186/s40337-024-01013-z

[30] Vogel M, Gil A, Galaz C, Urrejola P, Lacalle L, Jara R, et al. Virtually accompanied eating in the outpatient therapy of anorexia nervosa. Nutrients. 2023;**15**(17):3783

[31] Dane A, Bhatia K. The social media diet: A scoping review to investigate the association between social media, body image and eating disorders amongst young people. PLOS Global Public Health. 2023;**3**(3):e0001091

[32] Comité de Ética Clínica, Ciencias de la salud, Pontificia Universidad Católica de Chile. Characterisation and Follow-Up Study of a Sample of Patients Diagnosed with an Eating Disorder in the Outpatient and Inpatient Care of the UC-Christus Network. Chile: Comité de Ética Clínica, Ciencias de la salud, Pontificia Universidad Católica de Chile, ID 191021001, unpublished; ongoing study

Chapter 3

Bone Complications in Eating Disorders

Daniela Gómez and Pamela Pino

Abstract

Eating disorders (EDs), particularly anorexia nervosa (AN), are associated with serious bone complications, including low bone mineral density (BMD) and an increased risk of fractures. They affect both adolescents and adult women, which results in a BMD lower than the population average. Despite recovery, deficits in BMD may persist, highlighting the need for appropriate treatment strategies. Energy status, body composition, and neuroendocrine alterations play a crucial role in the bone health of these patients. Interventions such as estrogen replacement and anabolic treatments are promising, although further research is needed to optimize therapeutic strategies and improve the quality of life for affected individuals. This chapter provides an updated overview of bone complications in eating disorders and suggests innovative approaches for their management.

Keywords: anorexia nervosa, low bone mineral density, fractures, energy status, treatments

1. Introduction

Eating disorders (EDs) can lead to various medical complications, including osteoporosis, which may have lifelong debilitating consequences, particularly in anorexia nervosa (AN). These disorders are associated with significant neuroendocrine disturbances and low bone mineral density (BMD) [1]. Strict dieting, particularly during adolescence, can hinder the development of maximum bone density, potentially causing long-term skeletal complications.

Several studies have shown that both adult and adolescent women suffering from an *ED*, mainly *AN*, exhibit *BMD* below the population average, and of these, approximately 30% of adolescent and adult women with AN report having suffered at least one fracture [2–4, 9]. It is important to emphasize that both subtypes of *AN*—the restrictive subtype (*AN-R*) and the purging subtype (*AN-P*)—are associated with reductions in *BMD* and a higher risk of fractures—up to seven times higher—compared to control group [5, 6]. Both AN subtypes, restrictive and purging, are associated with lower BMD in the body, hip, and limb.

Additionally, we know that femoral neck *BMD* is lower in women with a history of *AN* compared to *controls*, even after an average of 21 years in recovery [7].

Meanwhile, patients with *bulimia nervosa* (*BN*) of normal weight have lower *spinal BMD* compared to *controls*, suggesting that weight loss is not the only factor contributing to the harmful effects of *ED* on bone health.

Despite their high prevalence, there is a lack of comprehensive guidelines for the diagnosis and treatment of these complications. Currently, the mainstays of treatment include weight restoration, the resumption of regular menstrual periods in women, and ensuring adequate levels of vitamin D and calcium. It is of utmost importance to develop effective treatments to increase *BMD* and reduce the risk of fractures due to the persistence of long-term deficits in patients with *ED*, particularly because studies suggest that deficits in BMD in *AN* persist despite recovery [8]. A population-based retrospective study found that the cumulative incidence of fractures in women with a history of AN was 57%, highlighting the significant pain and disability experienced by this group of patients.

This article addresses strategies for assessing outcomes in patients with *ED*, as well as factors contributing to altered bone metabolism and potential therapeutic approaches.

Pathophysiology, bone alterations, and fracture risk in anorexia nervosa: The etiology of reduced *BMD* in *AN* is multifactorial and is still under evaluation. Some patients with AN may have additional risk factors for low BMD in addition to their ED.

2. Factors mediating reductions in bone mass in patients with ED: Energy status and body composition

Numerous studies have shown that lower body weight and, in particular, reduced *lean body mass*, are key determinants of bone health in patients with emotional and behavioral disorders (EBD).

The subtypes of *AN* include the restrictive subtype (*AN-R*) and the purging subtype (*AN-P*), both of which are associated with reductions in *spinal BMD* and a higher risk of fractures compared to healthy controls [9]. *AN-R* and *AN-P* are also linked to lower total body, hip, and limb *BMD*, even in population-based samples, as demonstrated in a recent longitudinal study conducted in the United Kingdom [9]. On the other hand, patients with *BN* of normal weight have lower spinal bone mineral density compared to control groups, suggesting that weight loss alone may not fully explain the detrimental effects of an *ED* on bone health [10].

We know that *resting energy expenditure* has been related to bone remodeling, glucose homeostasis, and adipokines, underscoring the importance of preventing energy deficiency to limit hormonal disturbances and impairments in bone mineralization in *AN* [11].

Lower levels of body fat—especially subcutaneous fat—may also contribute, since this type of fat produces leptin, a hormone that supports bone growth.

Recent studies have focused on evaluating non-traditional fat reserves in *AN*, including marrow adipose tissue and *brown adipose tissue* (*BAT*). *White adipose tissue* (*WAT*) is specialized in storing chemical energy, while *BAT* dissipates energy as heat, and its presence is inversely correlated with age and body mass index (BMI). Women with *AN* have low *BAT*, which may be due to impaired thermogenesis as an adaptive mechanism to reduce energy expenditure in a state of energy deficit. Since women with *AN* have been observed to have higher levels of *preadipocyte factor 1* (*Pref-1*) compared to controls—which is inversely correlated with bone density [12]—it has been hypothesized that *BAT* may be involved in regulating the differentiation of stem cells toward the bone lineage at the expense of adipogenesis [13].

When a stromal progenitor stem cell differentiates into osteoblasts or adipocytes in the bone marrow, this process depends on the energy and hormonal environment of the marrow, and *marrow adipose tissue* is greater in women with *AN* compared to controls, and this is associated with lower measures of bone mineral density [14]. The degree of fatty acid saturation in bone marrow is also inversely correlated with bone mineral density, suggesting that saturated lipids may have negative effects on bone mineral density in *AN* [15]. This inverse relationship has also been observed in healthy individuals [16].

3. Nutrient intake

A recent study found that only 4 out of 30 patients with *AN* take multivitamin supplements, and 1 out of 30 takes calcium supplements [13, 17]. Low calcium levels have been linked to hypogonadal conditions that impact bone metabolism, as well as to vitamin D receptors, which play a key role in osteoblast activity.

In a recent cross-sectional study, serum *25-hydroxyvitamin D* (*25 OH-D*) levels below 50 nmol/L were positively associated with *spine bone mineral density Z-scores* in women with *AN*, as well as elevated levels of alkaline phosphatase, suggesting an adaptive osteoblastic reserve [18]. To date, there is no evidence to suggest that calcium or vitamin D supplementation increases bone mineral density in *AN*, and no correlation has been found between calcium or vitamin D intake and bone mineral density in adolescents with *AN* [18]. Nonetheless, an important objective of treatment is to ensure adequate intake of these nutrients in adolescent and adult women with ED.

Vitamin K supplements may, in turn, reduce *BMD* loss in women with *AN*, as adequate vitamin K intake is necessary for the gamma-carboxylation of osteocalcin. In individuals with AN-R, lower vitamin K intake is associated with higher serum levels of undercarboxylated osteocalcin. Vitamin K deficiency has been observed to be more pronounced in the purging subtype than in the restrictive subtype of *AN*, suggesting that further studies on vitamin K deficiency in other *ED* diagnoses are needed [19].

4. Endocrine alterations

In addition to weight loss, bone tissue is affected by various neuroendocrine disturbances, which can be observed in women with *ED*.

Suppression of the *hypothalamic-pituitary-gonadal (HPG) axis* conserves energy in a state of semi-starvation by preventing energy from being used for reproduction [20]. Estrogen normally inhibits osteoclastic bone resorption [21] and may also increase bone formation by inhibiting sclerostin and *Pref-1* [22, 23]. While estrogen deficiency is strongly associated with amenorrhea in individuals with AN, bone resorption is actually greater in amenorrheic adult women with AN than in postmenopausal women, indicating that additional factors are involved in the heightened bone loss seen in AN. Testosterone also has a positive effect on bones through its aromatization to *estradiol* (*E2*) and direct bone anabolic effects [24]. Women with *AN* have lower testosterone levels compared to controls, which are associated with lower *BMD* measures.

Regarding the *hypothalamic-pituitary-adrenal (HPA) axis*, it has been observed that adolescents and young women with *AN* have higher cortisol levels compared to controls, which are also detrimental to bone formation.

Hypercortisolism occurs in up to 80% of patients with *AN*. There is an increase in *corticotropin-releasing hormone* (*CRH*), which, in turn, stimulates *adrenocorticotropic hormone* (*ACTH*), leading to increased adrenal production of cortisol. Causes of hypercortisolism include stress from chronic nutritional deprivation, a compensatory mechanism to maintain euglycemia, increased ghrelin stimulating CRH, and reduced cortisol clearance. The consequences of hypercortisolism include decreased bone mass (inversely proportional to cortisol levels), inhibition of the *hypothalamic-pituitary-ovarian* (*HPO*) *axis*, and a deleterious effect on muscle mass. These elevated cortisol levels are also associated with increased truncal fat mass during weight recovery and may have a direct inhibitory effect on osteoblasts.

As a consequence of chronic energy and nutritional deprivation, *growth hormone* (*GH*) *resistance* emerges as an adaptive mechanism, characterized by low concentrations of *insulin-like growth factor* (*IGF-1*), despite high levels of GH [13, 17]. GH stimulates gluconeogenesis and lipolysis, helping to maintain normal blood glucose levels. On the other hand, low concentrations of *IGF-1*, an anabolic hormone, also promote energy conservation by reducing expenditure on longitudinal growth [18]. The increase in *ghrelin*, a potent secretagogue of GH, along with low insulin concentrations due to reduced intake, downregulates the hepatic expression of the *GH receptor* [9]. Additionally, the increase in *fibroblast growth factor 21* (*FGF-21*), which inhibits post-receptor GH transcription pathways [19], contributes to elevated GH levels, driven by both increased secretion and the frequency and amplitude of GH pulses. GH levels are inversely related to nutritional status, including *body mass index* (*BMI*), fat mass, and leptin levels [20]. This *GH resistance* and low circulating levels of *IGF-1* result in reduced longitudinal growth in patients with *AN* during puberty, and recovery is rarely complete [21–23]. This GH resistance is partially reversed with weight recovery [25], normalizing GH secretion and IGF-1 levels. Therefore, *AN* is associated with *nutritionally acquired growth hormone* (*GH*) *resistance*, characterized by lower *IGF-1* and higher GH concentrations compared to controls. Reductions in IGF-1 correlate with decreased bone formation markers and lower *lumbar spine BMD* [26]. Additionally, endogenous IGF-1 levels predict bone microarchitecture independently of BMI in women with *AN* [16]. In *AN*, higher GH levels are associated with lower IGF-1 and *fibroblast growth factor 21* (*FGF-21*) levels.

We know that appetite-regulating hormones, such as *leptin* (an anorexigenic hormone), *ghrelin* (an orexigenic hormone), and *peptide YY* (*PYY; anorexigenic*), are altered in *AN*. Leptin and ghrelin are bone anabolic, while PYY inhibits osteoblast differentiation. Compared to controls, adults and adolescents with *AN* have lower leptin levels, potential ghrelin resistance with higher ghrelin levels [27], and elevated PYY [28]. In healthy adolescents, higher ghrelin concentrations predict greater *BMD*. However, this association is not observed in *AN*, suggesting ghrelin resistance [29]. Decreased leptin levels and elevated PYY levels have been linked to lower bone turnover markers and reduced BMD [20]. On the other hand, *oxytocin* has anorexigenic and bone anabolic effects [30], and oxytocin levels are lower in women with *AN* compared to healthy controls, likely as an adaptive response, which is associated with lower *BMD* [31]. Osteoblasts, osteoclasts, and osteocytes have *serotonin* (*5-hydroxytryptamine* (*5-HT*)) *receptors* [32]. Only one study has shown that longer duration of selective serotonin reuptake inhibitor (SSRI) use is associated with lower BMD in young women with *AN*, even after controlling for time since diagnosis and duration of amenorrhea [33].

4.1 Strategies to assess bone changes in patients with ED

Most studies on *BMD* in the EBD population are limited by small study samples and narrow demographic data, e.g., male subjects are rarely included in studies. To evaluate the presence of bone changes in a patient with *ED* and determine whether these changes will affect the patient in the future, it is essential to conduct a thorough medical history, physical examination, and recommended laboratory evaluation for all patients with *AN*. Additionally, secondary causes of osteoporosis that could be influencing these patients should be assessed, particularly the use of medications, such as steroids, diuretics, selective serotonin reuptake inhibitors, and depot medroxyprogesterone acetate. *Dual-energy X-ray absorptiometry* (*DXA*) is a well-established tool for assessing fracture risk in postmenopausal women, although its predictive ability for fracture risk in premenopausal women with *AN* is not yet fully established [34]. An initial DXA scan is suggested for children and adolescents if amenorrhea has persisted for at least 6 months, and serial testing is recommended annually [35–37]. There are no specific clinical guidelines for adults with AN, but a DXA scan is recommended for any patient, regardless of gender, who has been hospitalized with an active eating disorder for 6 months or longer. According to the National Osteoporosis Foundation, follow-up screenings should be conducted every 2 years for adults.

In patients with *AN* whose condition has worsened or persists, repeating the DXA scan earlier may be indicated if the results would alter the course of treatment. Patients with malnutrition resulting from *avoidant/restrictive food intake disorder* (*ARFID*) or *BN* should also undergo DXA screening.

4.2 Potential treatment strategies

The first-line treatment for low *BMD* in *AN* is weight gain and the resumption of menstruation in female patients. Meta-analyses and systematic reviews examining the efficacy of weight recovery for improving BMD show favorable results [38–41]. Spinal BMD can increase by up to 3.1% with weight gain, although improvements may be slow and not detectable until after 16 months [39]. One study on women demonstrated that significant improvement in BMD was only observed if weight gain was substantial enough to lead to the resumption of spontaneous menstruation [42]. Weight gain appears to be the safest treatment for improving bone density in patients with *AN*.

It is known that patients with eating disorders have significantly lower serum levels of *25-hydroxyvitamin D* (*25 OH-D*) (a prohormone produced in the liver and the main circulating form of vitamin D) and *1,25 OH-D* compared to healthy controls, despite supposedly similar vitamin D intake [43]. Vitamin D is essential for ensuring the intestinal absorption of calcium and phosphorus, which are critical for the establishment of the bone matrix. One treatment strategy for patients with *ED* would be to maintain adequate vitamin D and calcium reserves in patients with low *BMD*, but there are conflicting data on what constitutes optimal vitamin D and calcium reserves, and no specific studies exist in the *ED* population. There is no evidence of improved BMD with vitamin D and calcium alone in patients with *AN*; however, one study showed a strong negative linear relationship between 25 OH-D levels in patients with *ED* and hip BMD [22].

Several other treatment strategies have been investigated in adolescent and adult women with *AN*, including the use of *oral contraceptives*, *physiological estrogen replacement with transdermal patches*, *testosterone replacement*, *dehydroepiandrosterone (DHEA)*, *insulin-like growth factor 1 (IGF-1)* (in combination with estrogen and progesterone), *bisphosphonates*, and *teriparatide*. Drugs combining *estrogen and progesterone* have not been shown to improve *BMD* in *ED* [44, 45], likely due to the IGF-1-reducing effect of oral estrogen. In contrast, physiological estrogen replacement, such as a 100 mcg *transdermal 17-beta estradiol patch*, which avoids first-pass liver metabolism, increases spine and hip BMD in adolescents with *AN*. A study found that girls with AN who underwent physiological estrogen replacement (with cyclic progesterone) for 18 months experienced greater increases in BMD compared to those who received a placebo, with their bone accumulation rates nearing those seen in healthy-weight controls.

This suggests that the type of estrogen used, the method of administration (transdermal versus oral), or both, may influence the treatment response.

Another study showed that a combination of *oral estrogen-progesterone* and *DHEA (50 mg daily)* for 18 months in young women with *AN* increased cortical thickness, improved femoral cross-sectional area [43], and maintained *DXA-measured BMD Z-scores* throughout the duration of the study [22].

In women with AN, weight gain is associated with increased testosterone levels, which are linked to improvements in BMD. However, low-dose transdermal testosterone treatment over 1 year did not lead to an increase in BMD in adult women with AN. On the other hand, short-term replacement of recombinant human insulin-like growth factor 1 (rhIGF-1) has been shown to enhance bone formation markers in both adults and adolescents with AN. In a placebo-controlled trial, when combined with estrogen-progesterone therapy, it resulted in increased spine and hip BMD in adult women with AN, compared to those who received no treatment.

Bisphosphonates are not recommended for women of reproductive age with *ED* due to limited knowledge of their long-term efficacy. After 1 year of *alendronate (10 mg daily)* administration in adolescents with *AN*, the *volumetric bone mineral density (vBMD)* of the femoral neck was higher in those who received alendronate compared to placebo controls. However, no effect was observed in the spine. In adults with AN, risedronate (35 mg weekly) has been shown to improve spine BMD over the course of 1 year. Teriparatide (TPT), a human parathyroid hormone (PTH) bone anabolic agent, has demonstrated proven efficacy in reducing fractures in postmenopausal women and men with osteoporosis.

A 21% increase in *BMD was recorded* and no recurrence of fractures after two years of teriparatide treatment in a 52-year-old patient with *AN* [6]. These findings were confirmed with a placebo-controlled randomized clinical trial, detecting a 6–10% increase in spine BMD after 6 months of teriparatide treatment (20 mcg daily) in older women with *AN*. However, safety concerns associated with TPT use stem from the increased risk of osteosarcoma in rodent studies, suggesting that TPT may not be suitable for young and adolescent women.

5. Conclusions

The significant, harmful, and long-term impact of *ED* on bone health underscores the importance of early and timely evaluation, as well as appropriate therapeutic strategies.

Gaining a deeper understanding of the neuroendocrine changes associated with *ED*, particularly *AN*, and their effects on *BMD* and bone microarchitecture opens up possibilities for future interventions in this group. Recent advancements in techniques for assessing *vBMD*, *BMD*, and bone microarchitecture have improved our ability to characterize bone impairments in women with *ED*. Physiological estrogen replacement has proven effective in increasing *BMD* in young women with *AN*, although full recovery remains elusive. Bisphosphonates, like risedronate, can enhance *BMD* in adult women with *AN* but should be used cautiously in women of reproductive age. The promising effects of teriparatide suggest it could be a future anabolic treatment for low *BMD* in older women with AN, though it is currently not suitable for young or adolescent women.

Understanding the underlying endocrine and nutritional mechanisms in patients with *ED* will enable a more effective approach to preventing and treating bone complications in this population.

Author details

Daniela Gómez[1,2*] and Pamela Pino[3]

1 Department of Psychiatry, University of Chile Clinical Hospital, Santiago, Chile

2 Interdisciplinary Care Center for Eating Disorders (AIDA), Santiago, Chile

3 Psychologist, Teaching and Research Unit, Interdisciplinary Care Center for Eating Disorders (AIDA), Santiago, Chile

*Address all correspondence to: dagomez@uchile.cl

References

[1] Fairburn CG, Harrison PJ. Eating disorders. The Lancet. 2003;**361**:407-416

[2] Misra M, Klibanski A. Anorexia nervosa and bone. The Journal of Endocrinology. 2014;**221**(3):R163-R176

[3] Miller KK, Grinspoon SK, Ciampa J, et al. Medical findings in outpatients with anorexia nervosa. Archives of Internal Medicine. 2005;**165**:561-566

[4] Faje AT, Karim L, Taylor A, et al. Adolescent girls with anorexia nervosa have impaired cortical and trabecular microarchitecture and lower estimated bone strength at the distal radius. The Journal of Clinical Endocrinology and Metabolism. 2013;**98**:1923-1929

[5] Nakahara T, Nagai N, Tanaka M, et al. The effects of bone therapy on tibial bone loss in young women with anorexia nervosa. The International Journal of Eating Disorders. 2006;**39**:20-26

[6] Fazeli PK, Klibanski A. Bone metabolism in anorexia nervosa. Current Osteoporosis Reports. 2014;**12**(1):82-89. DOI: 10.1007/s11914-013-0186-8

[7] Bachrach LK, Katzman DK, Litt IF, et al. Recovery from osteopenia in adolescent girls with anorexia nervosa. The Journal of Clinical Endocrinology and Metabolism. 1991;**72**:602-606

[8] Mueller SM, Immoos M, Anliker E, et al. Reduced bone strength and muscle force in women 27 years after anorexia nervosa. The Journal of Clinical Endocrinology and Metabolism. 2015;**100**:2927-2933

[9] Treasure J, Zipfel S, Micali N, Wade T, Stice E, Claudino A, et al. Bone mineral density, osteoporosis, and fractures among people with eating disorders: A systematic review and meta-analysis. International Journal of Eating Disorders. 2016;**49**(3):216-232

[10] Robinson L, Aldridge V, Clark E, et al. A systematic review and meta-analysis of the association between eating disorders and bone density. Osteoporosis International. 2016;**27**:1953-1966

[11] Maimoun L, Guillaume S, Lefebvre P, et al. Evidence of a link between resting energy expenditure and bone remodelling, glucose homeostasis and adipokine variations in adolescent girls with anorexia nervosa. Osteoporosis International. 2016;**27**:135-146

[12] Fazeli PK, Misra M, Goldstein M, et al. Fibroblast growth factor-21 may mediate growth hormone resistance in anorexia nervosa. The Journal of Clinical Endocrinology and Metabolism. 2010;**95**:369-374

[13] Eriksen SA, Prietzel H, Ibsen JR, et al. Bone and vitamin D status in patients with anorexia nervosa. Danish Medical Journal. 2014;**61**:A4940

[14] Bredella MA, Fazeli PK, Miller KK, et al. Increased bone marrow fat in anorexia nervosa. The Journal of Clinical Endocrinology and Metabolism. 2009;**94**:2129-2136

[15] Bredella MA, Fazeli PK, Daley SM, et al. Marrow fat composition in anorexia nervosa. Bone. 2014;**66**:199-204

[16] Paccou J, Hardouin P, Cotten A, et al. The role of bone marrow fat in skeletal health: Usefulness and perspectives for clinicians. The Journal of Clinical Endocrinology and Metabolism. 2015;**100**:3613-3621

[17] Chen J, Dosier CR, Park JH, et al. Mineralization of three-dimensional osteoblast cultures is enhanced by the interaction of 1α, 25-dihydroxyvitamin D3 and BMP2 via two specific vitamin D receptors. Journal of Tissue Engineering and Regenerative Medicine. 2016;**10**:40-51

[18] Soyka LA, Grinspoon S, Levitsky LL, et al. The effects of anorexia nervosa on bone metabolism in female adolescents 1. The Journal of Clinical Endocrinology and Metabolism. 1999;**84**:4489-4496

[19] Urano A, Hotta M, Ohwada R, et al. Vitamin K deficiency evaluated by serum levels of undercarboxylated osteocalcin in patients with anorexia nervosa with bone loss. Clinical Nutrition. 2015;**34**:443-448

[20] Misra M, Klibanski A. Endocrine consequences of anorexia nervosa. The Lancet Diabetes & Endocrinology. 2014;**2**:581-592

[21] Riggs BL. The mechanisms of estrogen regulation of bone resorption. The Journal of Clinical Investigation. 2000;**106**:1203-1204

[22] DiVasta AD, Feldman HA, Beck TJ, et al. Does hormone replacement normalize bone geometry in adolescents with anorexia nervosa? Journal of Bone and Mineral Research. 2014;**29**:151-157

[23] Faje AT, Fazeli PK, Katzman D, et al. Inhibition of Pref-1 (preadipocyte factor 1) by oestradiol in adolescent girls with anorexia nervosa is associated with improvement in lumbar bone 2013;**79** mineral density. Clinical Endocrinology.:326-332

[24] Miller KK, Meenaghan E, Lawson EA, et al. Effects of risedronate and low-dose transdermal testosterone on bone mineral density in women with anorexia nervosa: A randomized, placebo-controlled study. The Journal of Clinical Endocrinology and Metabolism. 2011;**96**:2081-2088

[25] Idolazzi L, El Ghoch M, Dalle Grave R, et al. Bone metabolism in patients with anorexia nervosa and amenorrhoea. Eating & Weight Disorders: EWD. 2016;**27**:1-7

[26] Liu JM, Zhao HY, Ning G, et al. IGF-1 as an early marker for low bone mass or osteoporosis in premenopausal and postmenopausal women. Journal of Bone and Mineral Metabolism. 2008;**26**:159-164

[27] Misra M, Miller KK, Kuo K, et al. Secretory dynamics of leptin in adolescent girls with anorexia nervosa and healthy adolescents. American Journal of Physiology-Endocrinology and Metabolism. 2005;**289**:E373-E381

[28] Misra M, Miller KK, Tsai P, et al. Elevated peptide YY levels in adolescent girls with anorexia nervosa. The Journal of Clinical Endocrinology and Metabolism. 2006;**91**:1027-1033

[29] Misra M, Miller KK, Kuo K, et al. Secretory dynamics of ghrelin in adolescent girls with anorexia nervosa and healthy adolescents. American Journal of Physiology-Endocrinology and Metabolism. 2005;**289**:E347-E356

[30] Tamma R, Colaianni G, Zhu LL, et al. Oxytocin is an anabolic bone hormone. National Academy of Sciences of the United States of America. 2009;**106**:7149-7154

[31] Lawson EA, Donoho DA, Blum JI, et al. Decreased nocturnal oxytocin levels in anorexia nervosa are associated with low bone mineral density and fat mass. The Journal of Clinical Psychiatry. 2011;**72**:1546

[32] Bliziotes M. Update in serotonin and bone. The Journal of Clinical Endocrinology and Metabolism. 2010;**95**:4124-4132

[33] Misra M, Le Clair M, Mendes N, et al. Use of SSRIs may impact bone density in adolescent and young women with anorexia nervosa. CNS Spectrums. 2010;**15**:579-586

[34] Bredella MA, Ghomi RH, Thomas BJ, et al. Comparison of DXA and CT in the assessment of body composition in premenopausal women with obesity and anorexia nervosa. Obesity. 2010;**18**:2227-2233

[35] Golden NH et al. Update on the medical management of eating disorders in adolescents. The Journal of Adolescent Health. 2015;**56**(4):370-375

[36] Golden NH, Abrams SA, Committee N. Optimizing bone health in children and adolescents. Pediatrics. 2014;**134**(4):e1229-e1243

[37] Misra M, Golden NH, Katzman DK. State of the art systematic review of bone disease in anorexia nervosa. The International Journal of Eating Disorders. 2016;**49**(3):276-292

[38] El Ghoch M, Gatti D, Calugi S, Viapiana O, Bazzani PV, Dalle Grave R. The association between weight gain/restoration and bone mineral density in adolescents with anorexia nervosa: A systematic review. Nutrients. 2016;**8**(12):769. DOI: 10.3390/nu8120769

[39] Franzoni E et al. Follow-up of bone mineral density and body composition in adolescents with restrictive anorexia nervosa: Role of dual-energy X-ray absorptiometry. European Journal of Clinical Nutrition. 2014;**68**(2):247-252

[40] Zipfel S et al. Anorexia nervosa: Aetiology, assessment, and treatment. Lancet Psychiatry. 2015;**2**(12):1099-1111

[41] Misra M et al. Weight gain and restoration of menses as predictors of bone mineral density change in adolescent girls with anorexia nervosa-1. The Journal of Clinical Endocrinology and Metabolism. 2008;**93**(4):1231-1237

[42] Veronese N et al. Vitamin D status in anorexia nervosa: A meta-analysis. The International Journal of Eating Disorders. 2015;**48**(7):803-813

[43] Gatti D et al. Strong relationship between vitamin D status and bone mineral density in anorexia nervosa. Bone. 2015;**78**:212-215

[44] Strokosch GR, Friedman AJ, Wu SC, et al. Effects of an oral contraceptive (norgestimate/ethinyl estradiol) on bone mineral density in adolescent females with anorexia nervosa: A double-blind, placebo-controlled study. Journal of Adolescent Health. 2006;**39**:819-827

[45] Misra M, Katzman D, Miller KK, et al. Physiologic estrogen replacement increases bone density in adolescent girls with anorexia nervosa. Journal of Bone and Mineral Research. 2011;**26**:2430-2438. DOI: 10.1002/jbmr.447

Chapter 4

A Meta-Analysis of the Efficacy of Exercise versus Cognitive Behavioral Therapy in the Treatment of Adults with Binge Eating Disorder

Chen-Jun Liu, Chen-Hang Yuan, Rui-Xin Huang, Li Zhao and Shan-Shan Mao

Abstract

This meta-analysis evaluates the efficacy of exercise vs. Cognitive Behavioral Therapy (CBT) in Binge Eating Disorder (BED), focusing on: binge eating frequency; Binge Eating Scale (BES); body composition (Body Mass Index, BMI); depressive symptoms (Beck Depression Inventory, BDI); and eating behavior patterns (Three-Factor Eating Questionnaire, TFEQ). Literature searched across PubMed, Web of Science, EBSCO, Cochrane Library, and Embase between January 1, 1996, and November 4, 2024. A random-effects model was used to calculate effect sizes (standardized mean difference (SMD)) and 95% confidence intervals (CIs). Seven studies with eight interventions involving a total of 473 participants were selected. 1. Compared with blank control group, exercise intervention group showed no BES improvement; BDI decreased (SMD = −0.42, p = 0.05) with small effect size; TFEQ showed large effect size for improved Cognitive Dietary Restraint (SMD = 1.06, p = 0.00), reduced Disinhibition (SMD = −1.06, p = 0.00), and Hunger (SMD = −0.63, p = 0.03). 2. Exercise + CBT reduced binge eating frequency (SMD = −1.04, p = 0.00) with large effect size vs. CBT alone. Conclusions: For BED patients, 1. Exercise alone showed benefits in reducing depressive symptoms (BDI) and improving specific diet-related psychological traits (TFEQ), it did not have effect on binge eating frequency, BES, or BMI. 2. (1) Exercise combined with CBT was better than CBT alone in reducing the binge eating frequency; and (2) the effects of exercise combined with CBT in BES, depressive symptoms, BMI or other dietary psychological domains were comparable to CBT alone.

Keywords: binge eating disorder, cognitive behavioral therapy, exercise interventions, mental health, meta-analysis

1. Introduction

Cognitive Behavioral Therapy (CBT) is currently recognized as the evidence-based psychological treatment for Binge Eating Disorder (BED), with proven efficacy in reducing binge episodes and alleviating comorbid symptoms, such as depression and anxiety [1–3] However, clinical research has also highlighted several limitations of CBT, approximately 20–60% of patients continue to experience residual symptoms after treatment, and dropout or relapse remains common [4–9]. Moreover, CBT's availability is often limited in rural or underserved areas, and psychological stigma may further reduce help-seeking behavior among patients [10–12].

Given these barriers, exploring adjunctive or alternative treatments such as exercise may provide accessible and effective options for individuals with BED [13]. Exercise, as a low-cost and widely accessible intervention, has been proposed as a promising adjunct to CBT, particularly in regions with limited access to mental health professionals [14–17]. Existing exercise intervention programs for patients with BED mainly include exercise modules in Behavioral Weight Loss (BWL) [14], Yoga [18], High-Intensity Interval Training (HIIT) [15], and Moderate Intensity Continuous Training (MICT) [19, 20].

Regarding the core symptom of Binge Eating Disorder (BED)—Binge Frequency (BF)—and its primary evaluation measure, the BES, HIIT has been shown to improve appetite regulation. However, some studies suggest that HIIT may also lead to increased overall food intake in individuals, potentially limiting its therapeutic efficacy for BED [21, 22]. In contrast, a 4-week low-intensity exercise intervention has been associated with significant reductions in binge eating symptoms, as indicated by decreased BES scores, along with improvements in eating-related psychopathology among individuals with BED [23]. Current evidence remains inconclusive as to whether exercise affects the severity of binge eating symptoms—and if it does, the nature and direction of that effect are still unclear.

BED is closely associated with obesity and physical inactivity. Although patients with BED are not necessarily associated with obesity, BED increases the risk of obesity-related complications [24–29]. However, the independent effect of exercise on BMI reduction in BED patients remains unclear. Empirical data from analysis comparing different et al. [30] and Jeffery et al. [31] consistently demonstrate that for obese BED patients, clinically significant weight management outcomes through exercise are achievable only when implemented in combination with CBT and structured nutritional management. Therefore, the impact of exercise alone on obesity outcomes in BED patients remains inconclusive and warrants further investigation.

Patients with BED frequently experience comorbid depressive symptoms [32, 33]. Regular exercise improves mental health in patients with BED and depressive symptoms, enhancing cognitive function [14, 34, 35]. Thus, the multidimensional benefits of exercise interventions hold promise as an ideal adjunct to CBT and may enhance long-term adherence to and efficacy of BED treatment. However, evidence on its independent effect in alleviating depressive symptoms in BED remains mixed. While Fossati et al. [30] suggest that exercise combined with CBT can reduce depression and improve mood, others report [36, 37] no additional benefit compared to CBT alone, highlighting the need for more rigorous research.

Despite accumulating evidence supporting the benefits of exercise on physical and mental health, its clinical application in BED remains debated. Given that the effects of exercise interventions on binge eating behaviors and psychological state in patients with BED are not yet clear, there is an urgent need to further validate the effects of the exercise interventions. This study systematically compares exercise and CBT for BED by assessing: (1) The evaluation [19] included binge eating frequency (reflecting binge eating symptom severity) and the BES (assessing behavioral patterns); (2) BMI [38] as body composition; (3) depressive symptoms as assessed by the Beck Depression Inventory (BDI) [39, 40]; and (4) TFEQ [41] for three psychological constructs related to food intake: Cognitive Dietary Restraint; Disinhibition; and Hunger. We aim to elucidate the potential effects of exercise intervention on the eating behaviors and psychological status of BED patients.

2. Methods

2.1 Study registration

The meta-analysis adhered to the procedures outlined in the Cochrane Handbook for Systematic Reviews of Interventions and was reported in compliance with the Preferred Reporting Items for Systematic Reviews and Meta-Analyses (PRISMA) guidelines. The review protocol for this study was registered in the PROSPERO (International Prospective Register of Systematic Reviews) database with the registration number CRD 42025646385.

2.2 Type of study

This is a meta-analysis examining the effects of CBT and exercise interventions in adults with BED, based on diagnostic manuals and validated tools. It is intended for the compilation of multiple randomized controlled trials (RCTs) into a Meta-analysis.

2.3 Study population

The inclusion criteria for the literature review encompass adults diagnosed with BED, with no restrictions on duration of illness, or case source.

2.4 Diagnostic criteria

Diagnostic and Statistical Manual of Mental Disorders, 4th Edition, Text Revision (DSM-IV-TR); Diagnostic and Statistical Manual of Mental Disorders, 5th Edition (DSM-V); and Binge Eating Scale (BES). Individuals diagnosed with BED based on validated tools (e.g., Eating Disorder Checkup) and/or judgment of a clinical specialist.

2.5 Intervention methods

The intervention group receives CBT and/or exercise interventions, including but not limited to aerobic training, resistance training, yoga either alone or in combination with other specified interventions and other forms of exercise. The control group receives either no intervention (blank control) or CBT. The intervention group duration is at least 1 month. Only randomized controlled trials (RCTs) were considered for inclusion.

2.6 Exclusion criteria

The exclusion criteria included studies that lacked specified outcome measures, duplicate publications, studies involving adolescents, non-interventional studies, trials that did not provide quantifiable exercise prescriptions, and those that focused solely on dietary modifications without incorporating exercise components. Studies of non-randomized controlled trials were also not included.

2.7 Outcome measures

Binge eating disorder symptoms' evaluation was assessed using different measures across the included seven studies with eight interventions: the Binge eating frequency was used in one study [42] and the BES was used in three studies [18, 19, 43]. BMI was used in four studies [18, 19, 42, 43]. Depressive symptoms were assessed using BDI across the included three studies [20, 30, 42]. TFEQ was used in one study [20].

2.8 Literature search strategy

A comprehensive literature search was conducted across multiple databases, including PubMed, Web of Science, EBSCO, Cochrane Library, and Embase. The search terms utilized were:

For interventions: "CBT OR exercise OR behavioral weight loss OR yoga OR other forms of exercise."

For BED: "binge eating disorder OR eating disorders."

The search was conducted using both subject headings and keywords. The search covered articles published between January 1, 1996, and November 4, 2024. Furthermore, the references of the selected articles underwent scrutiny to uncover pertinent studies.

2.9 Literature screening and data extraction

Two researchers independently conducted the literature search and screening process, based on the inclusion and exclusion criteria. Only articles with titles and abstracts directly pertinent to the aim of the review were advanced for further full-text screening. Discrepancies were resolved through discussion, negotiation, or consultation with a corresponding author. Data extraction was performed using EXCEL 2003, capturing the following information: (1) Basic information of the included studies: title, first author's name, publication year, etc. (2) Baseline characteristics of the study population: sample size, age, gender, etc. (3) Intervention details: methods, duration, etc. (4) Factors related to bias risk assessment: randomization methods, blinding, etc. (5) Outcome measures.

Efforts were made to address missing data by contacting the authors in order to obtain the necessary information. Unfortunately, despite these attempts, no additional data were received.

2.10 Evaluation of bias risk in included studies

The assessment of bias risk was conducted using the "Risk of Bias Assessment Tool" provided by the Cochrane Collaboration, encompassing the following key aspects: (1) adoption and description of methods for generating the randomization sequence; (2) whether allocation concealment was described; (3) whether blinding of participants was implemented; (4) whether blinding of data collectors and outcome assessors was achieved; (5) completeness of outcome data; (6) presence of selective reporting; and (7) other potential sources of bias. For each included study, judgments were made based on the aforementioned seven criteria, categorized as "Yes" (low risk of bias), "No" (high risk of bias), or "Unclear" (risk unknown). Funnel plots were employed to investigate potential publication bias across all outcome measures in the study series. Furthermore, sensitivity analysis was conducted to evaluate the influence of individual studies on the meta-analysis estimates. These assessments were graphically represented using Review Manager 5.4 to produce a risk of bias graph.

2.11 Statistical methods

Meta-analysis of the included studies was performed using Review Manager 5.4 software.

Heterogeneity between the included studies was evaluated using I^2 tests, with estimated p-values, performed in Review Manager 5.4 and Stata/MP 14. Heterogeneity was considered present when the p-value was <0.1, and $I^2 > 50\%$. Sensitivity analysis and subgroup analysis were conducted to identify potential sources of heterogeneity whenever detected. Despite these efforts, heterogeneity persisted, leading to the utilization of a random-effects model.

Funnel plots and Egger's test were employed to evaluate publication bias. These methods were utilized to ensure the integrity and reliability of the study's conclusions.

3. Results

3.1 Literature search process and outcomes

An initial search yielded 4432 records, encompassing multiple databases including PubMed, Web of Science, EBSCO, Cochrane Library, and Embase. After removing duplicates and applying inclusion and exclusion criteria, a total of seven studies with eight interventions met all inclusion criteria and possessed sufficient data for quantitative synthesis (meta-analysis). The studies focused on adults diagnosed with BED according to criteria from the Diagnostic and Statistical Manual of DSM-IV-TR, DSM-V, BES-validated instruments such as the Eating Disorder Examination, or clinical judgment by specialists. The literature screening process and outcomes are depicted in **Figure 1**.

3.2 Basic characteristics of included studies

The seven studies with eight interventions included in the meta-analysis comprised a total of 473 participants, with 365 in the treatment groups and 108 in the control groups. The treatment interventions primarily involved CBT and exercise interventions, while control measures consisted of waiting-list controls or treatment.

Three studies [19, 30, 42] compared exercise with CBT versus CBT and the other four studies [18, 20, 43, 44] compared exercise alone with no treatment. One study [20] included both men and women, and the other six studies [18, 19, 30, 42–44] had only women.

The general characteristics of the included studies are summarized in **Table 1**.

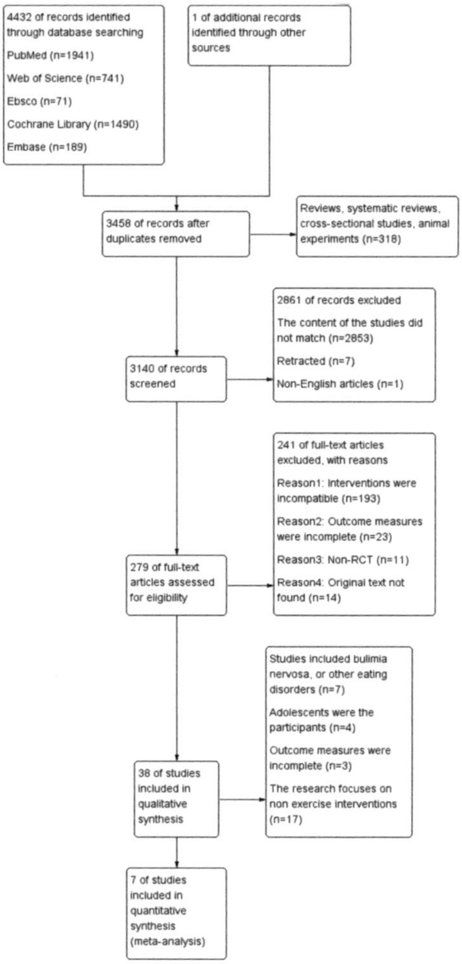

Figure 1.
Literature screening flowchart.

3.3 Quality and risk of bias assessment

Among the included studies, seven studies provided detailed descriptions of randomization methods, with only two studies reporting allocation concealment and three studies reporting blinding procedures. The quality and risk of bias assessments are presented in **Figures 2** and **3**. The Cochrane Collaboration's risk of bias tool was employed for RCTs, while other relevant quality assessment tools were used for observational studies. These assessments aimed to identify potential sources of bias and their impact on the study results, ensuring the robustness and reliability of the meta-analysis findings.

3.4 Meta-analysis results

Figures 4–8 present the results of the meta-analysis comparing different intervention modalities for various outcomes related to binge eating, BES, BMI, BDI, and TFEQ. The interventions included exercise compared to blank control and exercise combined with CBT compared to CBT.

First author & Year	Study Area	Diagnostic Criteria for BED	Number of Examples (n)	Age (Years)	Gender	Mode of Intervention	Duration of Intervention	Outcome Measures
Fossati 2004	Switzerland	EDI-2	CBT + EX group: n = 25 CBT group: n = 12 CBT + N group: n = 23	CBT + EX group: 37.4 ± 2.0 CBT group: 45.6 ± 2.9 CBT + N group: 42.3 ± 1.7	CBT + EX group: Female = 25 CBT group: Female = 12 CBT + N group: Female = 23	CBT + EX group: 12 times 90-minute CBT sessions per week, including physical activity recommendations. Three times a week, 30 minutes of physical activity, such as walking, swimming, or cycling. CBT group: 12 times 90-minute CBT sessions per week. CBT + N group: 2 times 90-minute CBT sessions per week, with a focus on dietetic learning.	12 weeks	BDI, BW, HAAD, HADD
Galasso 2020	Milan	DSM-IV + SCID	CBT + EX group: n = 10 CBT group: n = 9	CBT + EX group: 54 ± 11 CBT group 53 ± 13	CBT + EX group: Female = 10 CBT group: Female = 9	CBT + EX group: 4 times a week for 6 months, a total of 90 minutes including 60 minutes of aerobic exercise, 20 minutes of muscle strengthening exercises, and 10 minutes of relaxation. Three 90-minute CBT sessions per week. Dietary intervention was carried out according to the diet plan prescribed by the dietitian, and cooking activities were participated 2 times a week. CBT group: 3 times 90-minute CBT sessions per week. Dietary intervention was carried out according to the diet plan prescribed by the dietitian, and cooking activities were participated 2 times a week.	24 weeks	BES, BITE, BMI

First author & Year	Study Area	Diagnostic Criteria for BED	Number of Examples (n)	Age (Years)	Gender	Mode of Intervention	Duration of Intervention	Outcome Measures
Grilo 2022	Not Mentioned	DSM-5	EX + Placebo group: n = 35 EX + Naltrexone/ bupropion group: n = 35 Placebo group: n = 34 Naltrexone/ bupropion group: n = 32	EX + Placebo group: 46.00 ± 11.87 EX + Naltrexone/ bupropion group: 46.99 ± 12.98 Placebo group: 46.94 ± 12.57 Naltrexone/ bupropion group: 46. 03 ± 11.95	EX + Placebo group: Female = 28 Male = 5 Other = 2 EX + Naltrexone/ bupropion group: Female = 29 Male = 6 Placebo group: Female = 28 Male = 6 Naltrexone/ bupropion group: Female = 5 Male = 26 Other = 1	EX + Placebo group: 45 minutes of BWL treatment per week, moderate calorie reduction of 1500 kcal/ day, improvement of nutritional quality<30% fat and moderate physical activity 5 times a week for 30 minutes each time. EX + Naltrexone/ bupropion group: 45 minutes of BWL per week, naltrexone extended-release, 32 mg daily in combination with bupropion extended-release, 360 mg daily, 2 tablets twice a day. Placebo group: Placebo matches drug in appearance and frequency of administration. Naltrexone/ bupropion group: Naltrexone extended-release, 32 mg daily in combination with bupropion, 360 mg daily, taken twice daily, 2 tablets each time.	16 weeks	BDI, EDE, EDE-Q, HDL-C, HbA1c, LDL-C, TFEQ
Levine 1996	America	DSM-IV	EX group: n = 44 CON group: n = 33	36.6 ± 6.5	EX group: Female = 44 CON group: Female = 33	EX group: 3–5 walking exercises per week, with a weekly goal of consuming 1000 calories. CON group: Delayed treatment.	24 weeks	BDI, BW

First author & Year	Study Area	Diagnostic Criteria for BED	Number of Examples (n)	Age (Years)	Gender	Mode of Intervention	Duration of Intervention	Outcome Measures
Li 2024	China	BES	HIIT group: n = 15 Yoga group: n = 16 CON group: n = 16	HIIT group: 19.47 ± 0.74 Yoga group: 19.69 ± 0.874 CON group: 19.44 ± 0.63	HIIT group: Female = 15 Yoga group: Female = 16 CON group: Female = 16	HIIT group: 5 minutes of warm-up, 3 minutes of exercise at 90% VO_{2max}, 2 minutes of exercise at 50% VO_{2max}X, repeat 4 times, 3 times a week for 30 minutes each time for 8 weeks. Yoga group: 60 minutes, 3 times a week for 8 weeks. CON group: Daily activities.	8 weeks	BES, BMI, BW, FM, VO_{2max}
McIver 2009	Australia	BES	Yoga group: n = 25 CON group: n = 25	Yoga group: 40.1 ± 10.6 CON group: 42.0 ± 10.1	Yoga group: Female = 25 CON group: Female = 25	Yoga group: 60-minute yoga classes per week for 12 weeks. CON group: Wait 12 weeks for yoga treatment.	12 weeks	BES, BMI, IPAQ, Waist
Pendleton 2002	Australia, America	DSM-IV	CBT + EX group: n = 20 CBT + EX + MP group: n = 24 CBT group: n = 17 CBT + MP group: n = 23	45 ± 8.3	CBT + EX group: Female = 20 CBT + EX+ MP group: Female = 24 CBT group: Female = 17 CBT + MP group: Female = 23	EX group: 3 times a week, including 45 minutes each time, 2 cardio sessions per week and 1 home walk. MP group: 1 group activity every 2 weeks for 6 months. CBT group: 1 time per week for 90 minutes for 4 months.	16 weeks	BDI, BF, BMI

Note: BDI: Beck Depression Inventory; BES: Binge Eating Scale; BF: Binge Frequency; BITE: Bulimic Investigatory Test Edinburgh; BMI: Body Mass Index; BSQ: Body Shape Questionnaire; BW: Body weight; CBT: Cognitive Behavioral Therapy; CON: Control; DSM-IV: Diagnostic and Statistical Manual of Mental Disorders, 4th Edition; DSM-IV-TR: Diagnostic and Statistical Manual of Mental Disorders, 4th Edition, Text Revision; DSM-5: Diagnostic and Statistical Manual of Mental Disorders, 5th Edition; EDE: Eating Disorder Examination 17.0; EDE-Q: Eating Disorder Examination Questionnaire; EX: Exercises; FM: Fat mass; HAAD: Hospital Anxiety Scale; HADD: Hospital Depression Scale; HbA1c: Glycated Hemoglobin; HDL-C: High-Density Lipoprotein Cholesterol; IPAQ: International Physical Activity Questionnaire; LDL-C: Low-Density Lipoprotein Cholesterol; MP: Maintenance; SCID: Structured Clinical Interview; TFEQ: Three-Factor Eating Questionnaire.

Table 1.
Key characteristics of included studies.

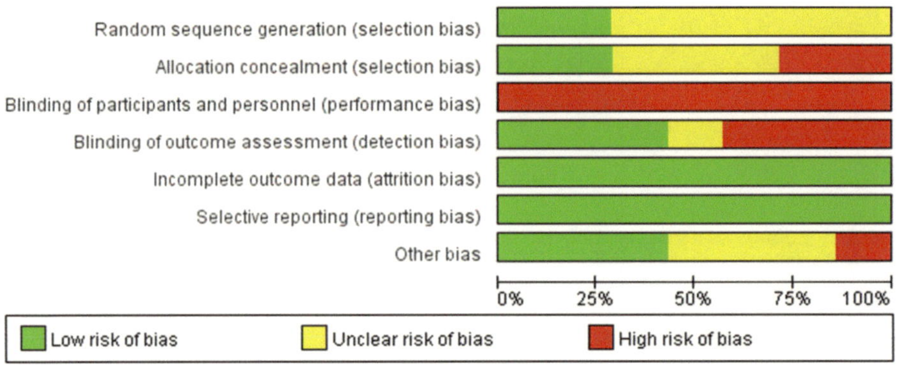

Figure 2.
Risk of bias assessment chart.

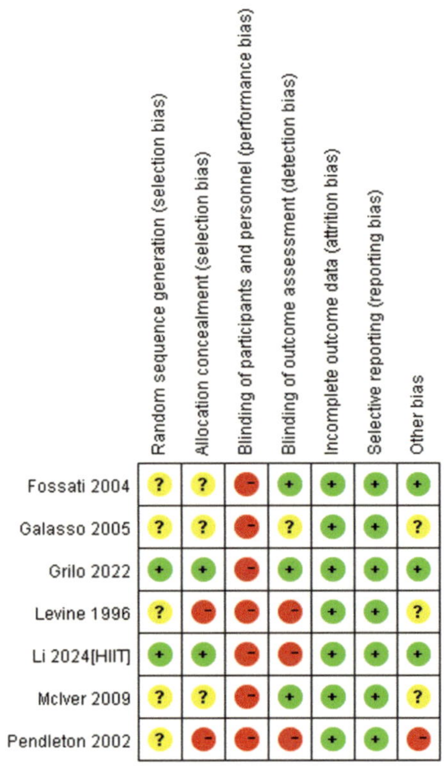

Figure 3.
Risk of bias summary chart.

3.4.1 Exercise intervention vs. blank control

Three randomized trials in two studies [18, 43] (n = 113) demonstrated no significant reduction in BES scores with exercise intervention compared to control conditions (SMD = −0.69, 95% CI [−1.86, 0.49]; p = 0.25). The analysis revealed critically high heterogeneity (I^2 = 88%), indicating substantial variations in treatment effects across studies that preclude definitive conclusions.

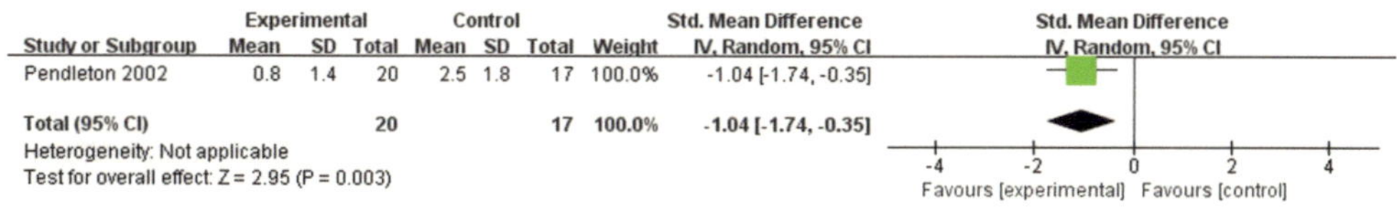

Figure 4.
Forest plot of Binge eating frequency.

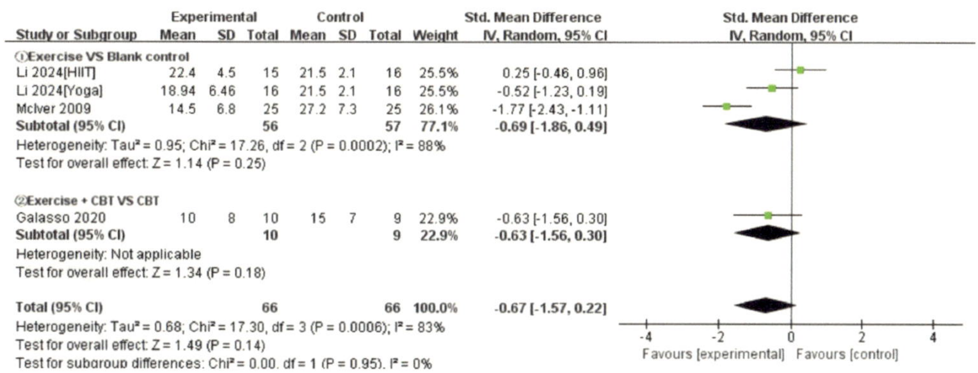

Figure 5.
Forest plot of BES.

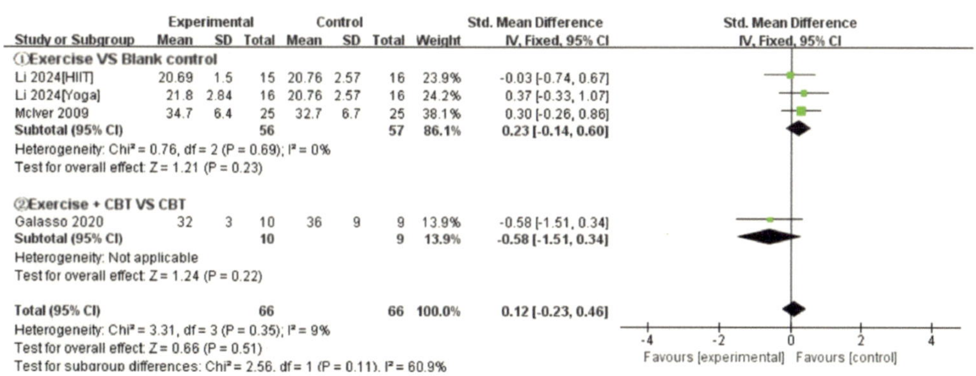

Figure 6.
Forest plot of BMI.

Three randomized trials in two studies [18, 43] with a total sample size of 113 participants demonstrated no significant reduction in BMI with exercise intervention compared to blank control (SMD = 0.12, 95% CI [−0.23, 0.46]; $p = 0.23$). The analysis revealed low heterogeneity ($I^2 = 0\%$), indicating consistent treatment effects across the included studies.

Two randomized trials [11, 20] ($n = 95$) demonstrated that exercise intervention produced a statistically significant reduction in depressive symptoms, albeit with a small effect size (SMD = −0.42, 95% CI [−0.83, −0.00]; $p = 0.05$). The analysis revealed minimal between-study heterogeneity ($I^2 = 0\%$), indicating consistent treatment effects across the included trials.

A single randomized study [20] ($n = 52$) demonstrated significant effects of exercise intervention versus blank control across all TFEQ subscales. The analysis

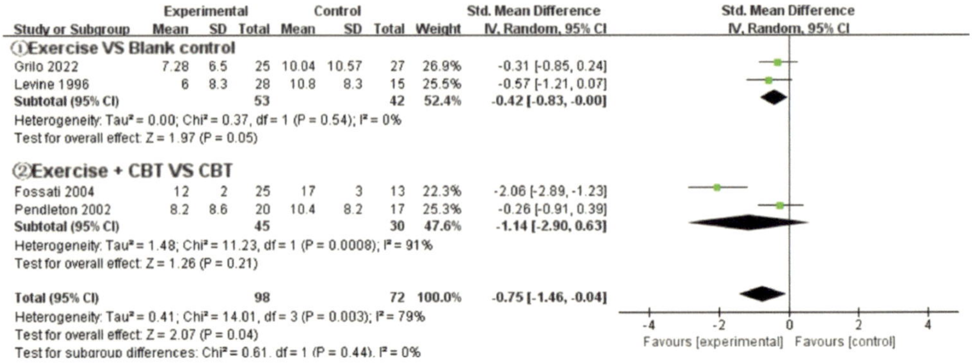

Figure 7.
Forest plot of BDI.

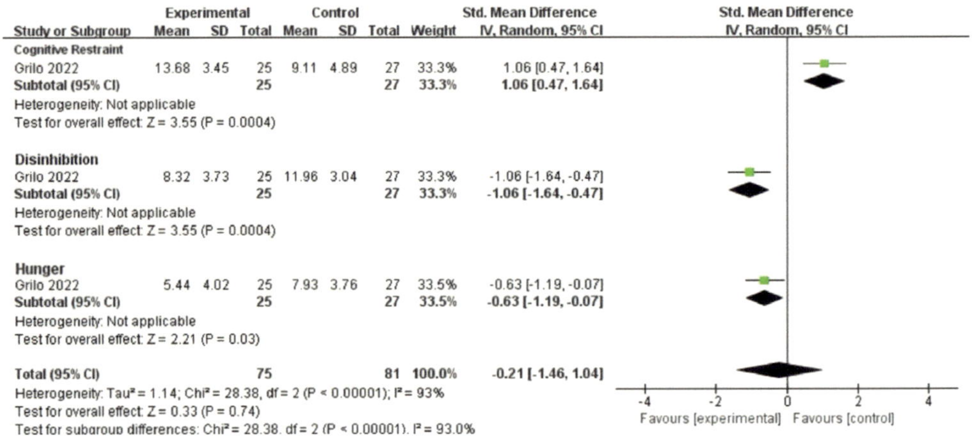

Figure 8.
Forest plot of TFEQ.

revealed: Cognitive Dietary Restraint: Large effect size improvement (SMD = 1.06, 95% CI [0.47, 1.64], $p = 0.00$); Disinhibition: Significant reduction with large effect size (SMD = −1.06, 95% CI [−1.64, −0.47], $p = 0.00$); and Hunger: Moderate reduction (SMD = −0.63, 95% CI [−1.19, −0.07], $p = 0.03$). Heterogeneity assessment was not applicable due to single-study design.

3.4.2 Exercise + CBT vs. CBT

A single randomized trial [42] ($n = 37$) demonstrated a statistically significant reduction in binge eating frequency following intervention (SMD = −1.04, 95% CI [−1.74, −0.35]; $p = 0.00$), representing a large effect size.

For the BES, one study [19] ($n = 19$) demonstrated no significant between-group difference (SMD = −0.63, 95% CI [−1.56, 0.30]; $p = 0.18$).

For BMI, one study [19] ($n = 19$) comparing exercise combined CBT versus CBT monotherapy demonstrated no significant between-group difference (SMD = −0.58, 95% CI [−1.51, 0.34]; $p = 0.22$).

Analysis of two randomized controlled trials [30, 42] ($n = 75$) found no statistically significant difference in depressive symptom reduction between exercise combined CBT and CBT alone (SMD = −1.14, 95% CI [−2.90, 0.63], $p = 0.21$).

3.5 Heterogeneity and possible publication bias

After eliminating studies with duplicate literature, mismatched interventions, inconsistent control groups, and incomplete or incorrect outcome indicators one by one, the remaining studies were analyzed by publication bias test. The funnel charts of the exercise intervention group versus the blank control group were observed; exercise intervention combined with CBT therapy versus CBT therapy, the charts were evenly distributed, no publication bias was found, and the results were stable.

Sources of study heterogeneity were analyzed by removing specific studies. For BES, removal of McIver et al. [43] reduced heterogeneity from $I^2 = 88\%$ to $I^2 = 56\%$. For BDI, removal of Fossati et al. [30] reduced $p = 0.21$ to $p < 0.00001$ after $p = 0.21$. These adjustments resulted in more consistent and reliable examination results.

4. Discussion

This meta-analysis examined eight interventions from seven studies, comparing the efficacy of exercise alone versus exercise combined with CBT for adult patients with BED. Exercise combined with CBT was better than CBT alone in reducing the binge eating frequency. Meanwhile, exercise alone was associated with improvements in depressive symptoms (BDI) and eating behavior dimensions (TFEQ), but it did not affect BES or body composition (BMI).

4.1 Exercise effects on binge eating frequency and binge eating behavioral patterns

Exercise combined with CBT vs. CBT alone demonstrated a large effect size in reducing binge eating frequency (SMD = −1.04), which aligns with prior research suggesting that CBT plus exercise may enhance treatment efficacy for binge eating symptoms [15, 30]. However, this finding should be interpreted with caution for several reasons. First, the effect of exercise alone could not be reliably assessed due to limited available data, as most studies did not report this outcome separately. More importantly, while statistically significant, this combined approach may lack substantial clinical significance, given that CBT alone has been well established as having core efficacy for binge eating behavior in numerous studies [12, 45, 46]. The additional benefit of incorporating exercise appears relatively marginal when considering the robust effectiveness of standalone CBT interventions.

Possible explanations for the superior efficacy of combined CBT and exercise in reducing binge eating frequency: (1) Exercise may enhance treatment adherence and engagement with CBT: Patients with binge eating disorder often experience low motivation, poor self-efficacy, and negative affect, which can hinder engagement with structured psychological treatments. Exercise interventions can improve self-regulation, mood, and perceived competence, potentially boosting motivation to engage in CBT sessions. Moreover, the incorporation of physical activity introduces routine, structure, and positive reinforcement, which may improve adherence to treatment protocols and reduce dropout rates. This behavioral scaffolding effect may help sustain the cognitive changes initiated by CBT [30]. (2) Reduction in binge-related emotional and physiological triggers through exercise: Exercise has been shown to attenuate psychological risk factors associated with binge episodes, including stress, anxiety [47, 48], and dysregulated affect. By reducing the frequency and intensity of emotional or physiological binge triggers, exercise may indirectly lower the likelihood of binge occurrences. This stress-buffering effect complements CBT's cognitive strategies, as patients may experience fewer internal cues (e.g., mood dysregulation) that require cognitive restructuring. Consequently, the combined intervention may result in more robust and consistent [39] symptom reduction than CBT alone.

Neither exercise alone nor exercise combined with CBT significantly improved BES scores, indicating their limited direct impact on disordered eating cognitions. This aligns with existing evidence [39, 49] regarding exercise's restricted effects on core BED symptoms. Three key factors may explain these null findings: (1) As BES specifically assesses maladaptive beliefs—cognitive domains primarily targeted by CBT—exercise-based interventions lack direct mechanisms for cognitive reappraisal [50–52]. (2) Substantial heterogeneity in exercise protocols (modality, intensity, duration) across studies may have obscured potential effects. (3) The BES instrument itself may be insensitive to capture short-term behavioral or affective changes induced by exercise.

4.2 Exercise effects on body composition

Neither exercise alone nor the combined intervention demonstrated significant effects on BMI in patients with BED. This null finding persists across various exercise modalities (aerobic and HIIT) and durations (8–24 weeks) [53, 54]. Several methodological factors may explain these results: (1) The absence of dietary control in most studies likely masked potential exercise-induced changes in body composition, as uncontrolled caloric intake could offset exercise-related energy expenditure. (2) The predominant focus on psychological outcomes in BED research has led to inadequate monitoring of dietary intake, making it difficult to isolate the specific effects of exercise. (3) While some previous studies [55, 56] reported body composition improvements with exercise, these may have implemented stricter dietary protocols than the interventions analyzed here. Future research should employ standardized dietary assessments [57] alongside exercise interventions to better determine whether exercise can influence BMI when dietary variables are properly controlled.

4.3 Exercise effects on depressive symptoms

A small reduction in depressive symptoms (BDI) was observed in the exercise group compared to blank controls (SMD = −0.42). This supports prior evidence suggesting exercise has antidepressant effects in BED: (1) Mechanistically, these improvements may be attributed to increased neurochemical activity (e.g., endorphins, serotonin) and behavioral activation [58, 59]. (2) Exercise facilitates behavioral activation by encouraging regular engagement in meaningful and rewarding activities, thereby interrupting the negative cycle of emotional avoidance and binge eating [15, 58–60].

In contrast, CBT operates through cognitive restructuring mechanisms. It focuses on identifying, challenging, and modifying maladaptive thoughts and core beliefs related to eating, self-worth, and body image [13]. This refers specifically to deep-seated maladaptive cognitive patterns, such as negative self-beliefs, distorted body image, or emotional reasoning—typically targeted by CBT through cognitive restructuring. CBT targets the cognition-emotion-behavior triad, aiming to directly correct distorted cognitive patterns that perpetuate depressive and binge eating symptoms [2]. However, the long-term effects of combined interventions remain unclear. Moreover, the observed high heterogeneity underscores the need for standardized exercise protocols—such as consistent frequency, type, and duration—to improve the reliability and comparability of future findings. Nonetheless, heterogeneity tests in this analysis showed no between-study variation ($I^2 = 0\%$), lending confidence to the robustness of the antidepressant effect of exercise interventions. While exercise effectively alleviates stress and improves mood, it may fail to address the cognitive distortions underlying binge eating behaviors.

4.4 Exercise effects on eating-related psychology

The Three-Factor Eating Questionnaire (TFEQ), developed in the 1980s [41], assesses Cognitive Dietary Restraint, Disinhibition, and Hunger. Exercise intervention alone led to significant improvements across all three dimensions, suggesting enhanced behavioral regulation over food impulses in individuals with BED.

- Cognitive Dietary Restraint—defined as deliberate strategies to control food intake [61]—improved significantly in one study ($n = 52$) comparing exercise to a blank control (SMD = 1.06, 95% CI [0.47, 1.64], $p = 0.00$), indicating enhanced dietary self-regulation. This reflects surface-level behavioral control rather than the maladaptive cognitions targeted by CBT. This suggests that exercise may promote healthier eating habits through structured behavioral changes, though it does not address the underlying psychological mechanisms of disordered eating that CBT is designed to modify.

- Disinhibition, referring to loss of control over eating due to internal or external cues [62, 63], also decreased significantly (SMD = −1.06, 95% CI [−1.64, −0.47], $p = 0.00$), suggesting that exercise may improve inhibitory control and reduce reactivity to food-related triggers. This effect may stem from exercise-induced improvements in self-regulation and stress resilience, though further research is needed to determine whether these benefits translate to long-term reductions in binge eating behaviors.

- Reductions in Hunger—defined as perceived hunger and its influence on intake [41, 64] —were moderate yet significant (SMD = −0.63, 95% CI [−1.19, −0.07], $p = 0.03$), supporting exercise's role in modulating hunger perception. These findings imply that regular physical activity may help stabilize appetite signals, potentially reducing susceptibility to overeating driven by heightened hunger cues.

These results support the potential role of exercise in modulating eating behaviors [65]. However, it should be noted that only one included study assessed the effects of exercise on eating behaviors using the TFEQ in individuals with BED. Therefore, the current evidence remains insufficient to draw definitive conclusions regarding the impact of exercise on TFEQ-measured Cognitive Dietary Restraint, Disinhibition, and Hunger in this population. Further research incorporating larger sample sizes and standardized assessments is needed to clarify the relationship between exercise and these specific eating-related psychological traits in BED patients.

5. Conclusions

For BED patients, 1. Exercise alone showed benefits in reducing depressive symptoms (BDI) and improving specific diet-related psychological traits (TFEQ: Cognitive Dietary Restraint, Disinhibition, Hunger), although it did not have effect on binge eating frequency, BES, or BMI.

2. (1) Exercise combined with CBT was better than CBT alone in reducing the binge eating frequency; and (2) the effects of exercise combined with CBT in BES, depressive symptoms, BMI or other dietary psychological domains were comparable to CBT alone.

6. Limitations

The variability in exercise mode, intensity, and duration across studies may have introduced heterogeneity that diluted the potential effects of the interventions. Different forms of exercise likely target varying aspects of physical and psychological health, making it challenging to capture a unified effect on binge eating symptoms. For instance, aerobic exercises may focus more on cardiovascular health, while resistance training might improve strength and body composition, and yoga could emphasize mindfulness and stress reduction. This diversity in approaches may result in different pathways of influence on binge eating behavior, which are not fully captured when analyzed collectively. Moreover, there are no articles where exercise is directly compared to CBT, and further research is needed to explore the relative efficacy of these interventions.

Second, the small sample sizes in several studies likely reduced the statistical power to detect significant effects. Many of the included studies may not have been adequately powered to identify subtle yet clinically meaningful changes in binge eating behavior. Small sample sizes increase the risk of Type II errors, where a potentially effective intervention is mistakenly deemed ineffective. Future studies would benefit from larger, adequately powered trials to increase confidence in the findings.

It is crucial that future research optimizes the design of exercise interventions. This could include tailoring exercise programs to target specific psychological mechanisms associated with binge eating, such as emotional regulation or impulse control. Additionally, standardizing exercise protocols with respect to intensity, frequency, and duration, and using more consistent outcome measures could help achieve more reliable and comparable results across studies. By addressing these methodological considerations, future research may be better positioned to identify the true potential of exercise interventions in mitigating binge eating behavior.

Acknowledgements

This research was supported by the National Key R&D Program of China (No. 2022YFC3600201) and Chinese Universities Scientific Fund (No. 2024JNPD001).

Conflict of interest

The authors declare no conflict of interest.

Author details

Chen-Jun Liu[1,2†], Chen-Hang Yuan[2†], Rui-Xin Huang[2], Li Zhao[1] and Shan-Shan Mao[1,2*]

1 Beijing Key Laboratory of Sports Performance and Skill Assessment, Beijing Sport University, Beijing, China

2 School of Sports Medicine and Rehabilitation, Beijing Sport University, Beijing, China

*Address all correspondence to: ss.mao@bsu.edu.cn

† These authors contributed equally to this work.

References

[1] National Collaborating Centre for Mental Health, National Institute for Health and Clinical Excellence: Guidance, in Eating Disorders: Core Interventions in the Treatment and Management of Anorexia Nervosa, Bulimia Nervosa and Related Eating Disorders. 2004, British Psychological Society (UK). Copyright © 2004, The British Psychological Society & The Royal College of Psychiatrists: Leicester (UK)

[2] Wilfley DE et al. A randomized comparison of group cognitive-behavioral therapy and group interpersonal psychotherapy for the treatment of overweight individuals with binge-eating disorder. Archives of General Psychiatry. 2002;**59**(8):713-721

[3] Wilson GT. Treatment of binge eating disorder. The Psychiatric Clinics of North America. 2011;**34**(4):773-783

[4] Mulkens S et al. To deliver or not to deliver cognitive behavioral therapy for eating disorders: Replication and extension of our understanding of why therapists fail to do what they should do. Behaviour Research and Therapy. 2018;**106**:57-63

[5] Waller G, Stringer H, Meyer C. What cognitive behavioral techniques do therapists report using when delivering cognitive behavioral therapy for the eating disorders? Journal of Consulting and Clinical Psychology. 2012;**80**(1):171-175

[6] Linardon J, Wade TD. How many individuals achieve symptom abstinence following psychological treatments for bulimia nervosa? A meta-analytic review. The International Journal of Eating Disorders. 2018;**51**(4):287-294

[7] Brown TA, Keel PK. Current and emerging directions in the treatment of eating disorders. Substance abus. 2012;**6**:33-61

[8] Linardon J, Hindle A, Brennan L. Dropout from cognitive-behavioral therapy for eating disorders: A meta-analysis of randomized, controlled trials. The International Journal of Eating Disorders. 2018;**51**(5):381-391

[9] Södersten P et al. Cognitive behavior therapy for eating disorders versus normalization of eating behavior. Physiology & Behavior. 2017;**174**:178-190

[10] Burns JM, Durkin LA, Nicholas J. Mental health of young people in the United States: What role can the internet play in reducing stigma and promoting help seeking? The Journal of Adolescent Health. 2009;**45**(1):95-97

[11] Crow SJ et al. A survey of binge eating and obesity treatment practices among primary care providers. The International Journal of Eating Disorders. 2004;**35**(3):348-353

[12] Carrard I et al. Randomised controlled trial of a guided self-help treatment on the internet for binge eating disorder. Behaviour Research and Therapy. 2011;**49**(8):482-491

[13] Fairburn CG et al. A prospective study of outcome in bulimia nervosa and the long-term effects of three psychological treatments. Archives of General Psychiatry. 1995;**52**(4):304-312

[14] Ashdown-Franks G et al. Exercise as medicine for mental and substance use disorders: A meta-review of the benefits for neuropsychiatric and

cognitive outcomes. Sports Medicine. 2020;**50**(1):151-170

[15] Batrakoulis A. Psychophysiological adaptations to yoga practice in overweight and obese individuals: A topical review. Diseases. 2022;**10**(4):107

[16] Aznar Laín S, Román-Viñas B. Physical exercise and sports in eating disorders. Nutrición Hospitalaria. 2022;**39**(Spec No2):33-40

[17] Herpertz S. Obesity is more than an eating disorder--the multidimensional perspective of a pandemia. Zeitschrift für Psychosomatische Medizin und Psychotherapie. 2008;**54**(1):4-31

[18] Li HM, Liu CJ, Shen YH, Zhao L, Yin CQ, Yu JG, et al. High-intensity interval training vs. yoga in improving binge eating and physical fitness in inactive young females. Scientific Reports. 2024;**14**(1):22912

[19] Galasso L, Montaruli A, Jankowski KS, Bruno E, Castelli L, Mulè A, et al. Binge eating disorder: What is the role of physical activity associated with dietary and psychological treatment? Nutrients. 2020;**12**(12):3622

[20] Grilo CM, Lydecker JA, Fineberg SK, Moreno JO, Ivezaj V, Gueorguieva R. Naltrexone-bupropion and behavior therapy, alone and combined, for binge-eating disorder: Randomized double-blind placebo-controlled trial. The American Journal of Psychiatry. 2022;**179**(12):927-937

[21] Sim AY et al. Effects of high-intensity intermittent exercise training on appetite regulation. Medicine and Science in Sports and Exercise. 2015;**47**(11):2441-2449

[22] Donati Zeppa S, Sisti D, Amatori S, Gervasi M, Agostini D, Piccoli G et al. High-intensity interval training promotes the shift to a health-supporting dietary pattern in young adults. Nutrients. 2020;**12**(3):843

[23] Duarte C, Pinto-Gouveia J, Stubbs RJ. Compassionate attention and regulation of eating behaviour: A pilot study of a brief low-intensity intervention for binge eating. Clinical Psychology and Psychotherapy. 2017;**24**(6):O1437-o1447

[24] Sherwood NE, Jeffery RW, Wing RR. Binge status as a predictor of weight loss treatment outcome. International Journal of Obesity and Related Metabolic Disorders. 1999;**23**(5):485-493

[25] Vancampfort D et al. Health related quality of life, physical fitness and physical activity participation in treatment-seeking obese persons with and without binge eating disorder. Psychiatry Research. 2014;**216**(1):97-102

[26] Hudson JI et al. The prevalence and correlates of eating disorders in the National Comorbidity Survey Replication. Biological Psychiatry. 2007;**61**(3):348-358

[27] Javaras KN et al. Co-occurrence of binge eating disorder with psychiatric and medical disorders. The Journal of Clinical Psychiatry. 2008;**69**(2):266-273

[28] Yager J. Binge eating disorder: The search for better treatments. The American Journal of Psychiatry. 2008;**165**(1):4-6

[29] Grilo CM, Masheb RM, Wilson GT. Efficacy of cognitive behavioral therapy and fluoxetine for the treatment of binge eating disorder: A randomized double-blind placebo-controlled comparison. Biological Psychiatry. 2005;**57**(3):301-309

[30] Fossati M, Amati F, Painot D, Reiner M, Haenni C, Golay A. Cognitive-behavioral therapy with simultaneous nutritional and physical activity education in obese patients with binge eating disorder. Eating and Weight Disorders. 2004;**9**(2):134-138

[31] Jeffery RW et al. Monetary contracts in weight control: Effectiveness of group and individual contracts of varying size. Journal of Consulting and Clinical Psychology. 1983;**51**(2):242-248

[32] Vancampfort D et al. A systematic review on physical therapy interventions for patients with binge eating disorder. Disability and Rehabilitation. 2013;**35**(26):2191-2196

[33] Galasso L et al. Aerobic exercise training improves physical performance of patients with binge-eating disorder. Sport Sciences for Health. 2018;**14**(1):47-51

[34] da Luz FQ, Hay P, Touyz S, Sainsbury A. Obesity with comorbid eating disorders: Associated health risks and treatment approaches. Nutrients. 2018;**10**(7):829

[35] Raisi A et al. Treating binge eating disorder with physical exercise: A systematic review and meta-analysis. Journal of Nutrition Education and Behavior. 2023;**55**(7):523-530

[36] Devlin MJ et al. Cognitive behavioral therapy and fluoxetine as adjuncts to group behavioral therapy for binge eating disorder. Obesity Research. 2005;**13**(6):1077-1088

[37] Berkman ND et al. AHRQ comparative effectiveness reviews. In: Management and Outcomes of Binge-Eating Disorder. Rockville (MD): Agency for Healthcare Research and Quality (US); 2015

[38] Schag K et al. IMPULS: Impulsivity-focused group intervention to reduce binge eating episodes in patients with binge eating disorder - A randomised controlled trial. Psychotherapy and Psychosomatics. 2019;**88**(3):141-153

[39] Mathisen TF et al. Is physical exercise and dietary therapy a feasible alternative to cognitive behavior therapy in treatment of eating disorders? A randomized controlled trial of two group therapies. The International Journal of Eating Disorders. 2020;**53**(4):574-585

[40] Peterson CB et al. Predictors of treatment outcome for binge eating disorder. The International Journal of Eating Disorders. 2000;**28**(2):131-138

[41] Stunkard AJ, Messick S. The three-factor eating questionnaire to measure dietary restraint, disinhibition and hunger. Journal of Psychosomatic Research. 1985;**29**(1):71-83

[42] Pendleton VR, Goodrick GK, Poston WS, Reeves RS, Foreyt JP. Exercise augments the effects of cognitive-behavioral therapy in the treatment of binge eating. The International Journal of Eating Disorders. 2002;**31**(2):172-184

[43] McIver S, O'Halloran P, McGartland M. Yoga as a treatment for binge eating disorder: A preliminary study. Complementary Therapies in Medicine. 2009;**17**(4):19632546, 196-202

[44] Levine MD, Marcus MD, Moulton P. Exercise in the treatment of binge eating disorder. The International Journal of Eating Disorders. 1996;**19**(2):171-177

[45] DeBar LL et al. Guided self-help treatment for recurrent binge eating: Replication and extension. Psychiatric Services. 2011;**62**(4):367-373

[46] Grilo CM, Masheb RM. A randomized controlled comparison of guided self-help cognitive behavioral therapy and behavioral weight loss for binge eating disorder. Behaviour Research and Therapy. 2005;**43**(11):1509-1525

[47] Pearce M et al. Association between physical activity and risk of depression: A systematic review and meta-analysis. JAMA Psychiatry. 2022;**79**(6):550-559

[48] Schuch FB, Stubbs B. The role of exercise in preventing and treating depression. Current Sports Medicine Reports. 2019;**18**(8):299-304

[49] Quesnel DA et al. Medical and physiological complications of exercise for individuals with an eating disorder: A narrative review. Journal of Eating Disorders. 2023;**11**(1):3

[50] Giel KE et al. Binge eating disorder. Nature Reviews. Disease Primers. 2022;**8**(1):16

[51] Kessler RM et al. The neurobiological basis of binge-eating disorder. Neuroscience and Biobehavioral Reviews. 2016;**63**:223-238

[52] Moghimi E, Davis C, Bonder R, Knyahnytska Y, Quilty L. Exploring women's experiences of treatment for binge eating disorder: Methylphenidate vs. cognitive behavioural therapy. Progress in Neuro-Psychopharmacology and Biological Psychiatry. 2022;**114**:110492

[53] Cena H et al. Benefits of exercise in multidisciplinary treatment of binge eating disorder in adolescents with obesity. International Journal of Environmental Research and Public Health. 2022;**19**(14)

[54] Lydecker JA et al. Preoccupation in bulimia nervosa, binge-eating disorder, anorexia nervosa, and higher weight. The International Journal of Eating Disorders. 2022;**55**(1):76-84

[55] Batrakoulis A. Role of mind-body fitness in obesity. Diseases. 2022;**11**(1):1

[56] Batrakoulis A. Psychophysiological adaptations to pilates training in overweight and obese individuals: A topical review. Diseases. 2022;**10**(4):71

[57] Foster E et al. Validity and reliability of an online self-report 24-h dietary recall method (Intake24): A doubly labelled water study and repeated-measures analysis. Journal of Nutritional Science. 2019;**8**:e29

[58] Kandola A et al. Physical activity and depression: Towards understanding the antidepressant mechanisms of physical activity. Neuroscience and Biobehavioral Reviews. 2019;**107**:525-539

[59] Smith PJ, Merwin RM. The role of exercise in management of mental health disorders: An integrative review. Annual Review of Medicine. 2021;**72**:45-62

[60] Imboden C et al. Aerobic exercise or stretching as add-on to inpatient treatment of depression: Similar antidepressant effects on depressive symptoms and larger effects on working memory for aerobic exercise alone. Journal of Affective Disorders. 2020;**276**:866-876

[61] King NA et al. Exercise, appetite and weight management: Understanding the compensatory responses in eating behaviour and how they contribute to variability in exercise-induced weight loss. British Journal of Sports Medicine. 2012;**46**(5):315-322

[62] Schaumberg K et al. Does short-term fasting promote pathological

eating patterns? Eating Behaviors. 2015;**19**:168-172

[63] Schaumberg K, Anderson DA. Does short-term fasting promote changes in state body image? Body Image. 2014;**11**(2):167-170

[64] Bryant EJ et al. Obesity and eating disturbance: The role of TFEQ restraint and disinhibition. Current Obesity Reports. 2019;**8**(4):363-372

[65] Kruger R, De Bray JG, Beck KL, Conlon CA, Stonehouse W. Exploring the relationship between body composition and eating behavior using the three factor eating questionnaire (TFEQ) in young New Zealand women. Nutrients. 2016;**8**(7):386

Chapter 5

Mentalization and Personality: What Is Their Role in the Unfolding of Eating Disorders in Adolescents and Young Adults?

Giulia Gagliardini and Antonello Colli

Abstract

Mentalization represents the mental process by which individuals make sense of their own and others' behaviors in terms of intentional mental states. Mentalization is a capacity that is impaired in different psychopathological domains, such as eating disorders (EDs) and personality disorders (PDs). Mentalization and personality both have been hypothesized to play a crucial role in the unfolding of EDs. However, the nature of this relationship remains far from clear. In this chapter, we aim to critically discuss the roles of mentalization and personality in the unfolding of ED pathology, with a specific focus on the population of young adults that is critically at risk for mental health problems. We will discuss previous studies on the presence of specific personality and mentalizing profiles in EDs.

Keywords: mentalization, eating disorders, personality, young adults, reflective function

1. Introduction

Eating disorders (EDs) are mental disorders that are characterized by distortions in eating behaviors associated with distress. The most commonly diagnosed EDs in adulthood are anorexia nervosa (AN), bulimia nervosa (BN), and binge eating disorder (BED), which are characterized by different eating behaviors. To sum up ED characteristics, anorexia nervosa (AN) has among its core features the fear of gaining weight with a disturbance in the way the individual experiences their body weight and/or shape, along with a restrictive eating pattern. This leads to significant weight loss or being underweight. AN subtypes are anorexia nervosa restricting type (AN-R) and anorexia nervosa binge eating/purge type (AN-BP). AN-BP is characterized by recurrent episodes of binge eating and/or purging behavior. Bulimia nervosa (BN) is characterized by binge eating, followed by compensatory behaviors, such as self-induced vomiting. Binge eating disorder (BED) is characterized by binge eating without subsequent compensatory behavior. Other specified feeding or eating disorders

(OSFEDs) are diagnosed when ED symptomatology is present but the person does not meet all symptom criteria for either AN, BN, or BED [1].

In recent years, the presence of specific different subtypes (e.g. AN-R, AN-BP, and BN) has been criticized since there is still conflicting evidence on the possibility of discriminating between those patients in a clinically relevant and significant way, especially when considering AN-BP and BN. Moreover, some authors have previously pointed out that "as with many other classes of psychiatric disorders," use of the "other specified feeding or eating disorder" is a prevalent diagnosis when the fifth edition of the Diagnostic and Statistical Manual of Mental Disorders (DSM-5) is used" ([2], pp. 249–250).

EDs are also characterized by different phenomena related to the diagnosis that can be summed up into two issues:

1. the crossover of symptoms over time and

2. the high presence of comorbidity.

In relation to the first issue, we must note that EDs tend to fluctuate over time, with a patient with AN that could develop (or turn to) BN over time, or to binge episodes without compensating behaviors. A different but related issue concerns the possibility of a non-ED symptom-shifting path, meaning that patients with an ED could, with time, have different symptoms or disorders that are not related to EDs but to different psychopathological domains (such as self-harming behaviors). This possibility has been investigated, among others, by Garke and colleagues [3], who conducted a study on a sample of 3159 adults and young adults (the mean age of the sample was 26 years old). The authors found that 13% of the sample could be identified as a "symptom shifter", with a decrease in at least one ED symptom and an increase in a non-ED symptom over the last year.

Non-ED symptoms considered in the study were, for example, self-harm and substance use disorder. Patients who experienced symptom shifts had overall higher levels of ED pathology. Moreover, as found by the authors, symptom shifters "had significantly higher ratings than nonshifters, on the following variables related to mental illness at baseline: anxiety, depression, compulsivity, deliberate self-harm, impairment due to eating disorder symptoms, and lower ratings in clinician rated functioning. At follow-up, symptom shifters had significantly higher ratings than nonshifters on the following variables: anxiety, depression, compulsivity, emotion dysregulation, ADHD symptoms, deliberate self-harm, impairment due to eating disorder symptoms, as well as lower ratings in clinician rated function. This indicates that symptom shifters had an overall higher level of symptoms as well as a greater functional impairment than nonshifters, an association that was attenuated at follow-up (demonstrated by consistently larger effect-sizes)" ([3], p. 590).

One of the major issues in relation to ED pathology and treatment is related to the fact that EDs often have a wide range of comorbid disorders, including personality disorders (PDs), anxiety and mood disorders, and substance use disorder. This could be related to processes that impact on all the different phenomenological outcomes, such as mentalization or specific personality traits.

The relationship between EDs and personality pathology has so far been investigated in previous studies, and this will be critically reviewed in this chapter.
ED symptoms have been hypothesized to be an emerging product of patients'

personality, and mentalization could also play a role in the unfolding of ED symptoms. Mentalization, in fact, also represents a valuable variable that can help us better understand the complex relationship between ED pathology and comorbidities [4]. We will posit that both personality and mentalization can play a crucial role in the unfolding of EDs, and could help us overcome some of the aforementioned diagnostic and clinical issues when treating EDs. Providing the most accurate diagnosis of our patients is crucial for the tailoring of the interventions and represents a major issue when working with EDs.

In relation to psychological disorders and specifically to ED diagnosis, we have seen that there are different concerns in the current literature. In fact, it is becoming increasingly important to develop tailored and specific diagnoses that can reflect the individual pathway to the disease. As Barron [5] has argued, it is important to make diagnoses meaningful, to understand which specific factors can affect psychopathology in order to develop tailored and effective treatments for each patient and to respect the complexity of each therapeutic dyadic encounter [6, 7]. We propose that including, within the diagnoses of EDs that are available in the literature, a specific section on personality and mentalization could increase their clinical value. In relation to this proposal, personality and mentalization problematics should not, in our opinion, be considered as possible comorbidities and co-occurring symptoms, but as processes that characterize the ED diagnosis.

2. The role of personality in eating disorder behavior

The role of personality in EDs has been previously investigated in different publications in the last 30 years and more (e.g. [8]). In more recent years, Martinussen et al. [9] conducted a meta-analysis of 87 studies from 17 different countries, which demonstrated that PDs were more present in people with EDs, for whom the mean proportion of PDs was .52, compared to healthy controls, for whom the mean proportion of PDs was .09. The most represented Cluster in ED patients was Cluster C, and in relation to specific PDs, the authors found that paranoid, borderline, avoidant, dependent and obsessive-compulsive PDs were the most common PDs in the considered ED samples. The aforementioned study found that "eating disorders with personality disorders are characterized by chronicity and low levels of functioning compared with eating disorders without personality disorders" ([8], p. 403), thus representing a major clinical issue in everyday practice.

Previous studies on the relationship between EDs and personality pathology, in which personality pathology was assessed using a categorical approach, have found that personality can explain meaningful variance in the onset, course, and outcome of EDs. However, as Solomon-Krakus and colleagues [2] have stated, "results from three meta-analyses examining the role of personality in EDs reveal a set of inconsistent findings across studies. One possible explanation for this lack of consistency is that most studies examining personality have used categorical methods to assess EDs, and few studies have used dimensional assessments of both normal range personality and/or personality psychopathology." [p. 249]. When adopting a dimensional approach to EDs, different and further stimulating results have been found.

In our opinion, and in light of the aforementioned studies, personality problems should be considered not only as potentially comorbid but as integrative facets of ED pathology. Disconnecting personality and ED diagnoses may prevent tailoring the assessment in a clinically useful way.

2.1 Personality and eating behaviors: A dimensional approach

Different studies have investigated the relationship between specific personality characteristics and EDs, and Westen and Harnden-Fischer [10] in their work found three personality subtypes that cut across ED diagnoses:

1. a dysregulated/under-controlled pattern characterized by emotional inhibition, cognitively sparse representations of the self and others, and interpersonal avoidance;

2. a high-functioning/perfectionistic pattern characterized by psychological strengths, alloyed with perfectionism and negative affectivity [11];

3. a constricted/overcontrolled group characterized by difficulty expressing anger, desires, and impulses [10].

In 2005, Thompson-Brenner and Westen [11] investigated the possible presence of these personality profiles in 145 female[1] bulimic patients with a mean age of 28 years old (SD = 10.2). The authors asked a sample of 145 therapists to provide information on their patients' ED symptoms and personality characteristics. The authors found that the majority of the sample (84%) could fit into the above-described personality profiles, with 42% of the patients belonging to the high-perfectionist profile, 31% to the constricted profile and 27% to the dysregulated profile.

On a side note, and supporting the problems in ED diagnosis mentioned above, "with respect to lifetime diagnoses, and consistent with data on eating disorder diagnostic 'crossover' using structured interviews (Eddy et al., 2002), clinicians reported that 38% of the patients had met criteria for the diagnosis of anorexia nervosa at some point" ([11], p. 518). The three different profiles were related to different psychopathological domains, with the dysregulated group being the one with the major impairments and comorbid clinical and personality disorders This points toward the necessity to look at those processes as part of the same psychopathological core feature of EDs, and to increase the usefulness of ED diagnoses by including personality impairments in their description.

When adopting a dimensional approach, one of the most studied theories is the Five Factor Model (FFM), which posits that personality represents the interplay of five different dimensions: openness, conscientiousness, neuroticism, extraversion, and agreeableness. Each of these dimensions is composed of different sub-dimensions, for example, some of the facets of extraversion considered also for research purposes are kindness, activity and excitement-seeking. Different studies have investigated the role of FFM personality traits and eating pathology.

In 2022, Gilmartin and colleagues published a study on "the FFM and the possibility of using it to predict eating pathology among adolescents and young adults. The study involved 394 females and 167 males aged between 16 and 30 years of age.

---

[1] Most of the research on EDs is focused on women, and this sample as all the other samples presented in this work reflect this limitation. We will discuss this issue in the Conclusions section of this chapter.

Their work found differences in males and females in relation to the analyzed processes[2]. Specifically, in relation to females, a profile of depressed and restrained personality traits along with a tendency to be younger in age and concerned with weight and shape was associated with restrained eating" ([12], p. 149). This study suggested that age had a role on the relationship between personality traits and eating behaviors, implying that adolescents and young adults represent a specific population that has to be investigated in their specificities and with studies focused on the specific patterns of relationship between EDs and personality, also considering the specific transitions that those age spans imply.

In conclusion, a more accurate description of ED pathology should include a reflection on the influence that age can have on the unfolding of the diseases in order to move toward a more precise diagnostic approach. Studies such as the one mentioned above have enlightened how age and personality dimensions can impact ED features such as weight concerns—Risk profiles for EDs should include these features, above and beyond the potentially comorbid categorical PD diagnosis.

3. Mentalization

Mentalization represents the mental process that allows us to perceive and interpret our own and others' behaviors in terms of intentional mental states such as beliefs and desires [13]. This psychological function is believed to have a crucial role in the unfolding of different psychopathological domains, such as personality disorders (PDs) and eating disorders (EDs). In this section, we will dig into the relationship between EDs and personality and mentalization, with a specific focus on the populations of adolescents and young adults.

Mentalization represents the mental process by which we perceive and interpret our own and other people's behaviors in terms of intentional mental states, such as beliefs, desires, and thoughts [13].

The capacity to mentalize is the product of the dynamic interplay between eight different dimensions organized as opposite poles (polarities) of experience:

1. Self versus others.

2. Cognitive versus affective.

3. Internal versus external.

4. Implicit versus explicit.

The self/other polarity refers to the object of mentalization: Mentalizing, in fact, can be directed toward our own or others' behaviors and thoughts. We must imagine

[2] The authors found several differences related to gender. In relation to purging behaviors, for example, and in line with different research, males were found to be described as "agitated with difficulties asserting themselves with others" (p. 150) while purging females were "impulsive and uncontrolled" (p. 150). Moreover, "body image dissatisfaction was found to mediate the relationship between purging and a tendency to be reserved in males and overly soft with others among females" (p. 151). It is, however, beyond the scope of this work to analyze the differences between the male and female populations.

these poles as dynamically intertwined and can be reciprocally influenced. An example is when we use our own experience to understand others ("I would have felt terrible in this situation, and I can somehow imagine how this could make him feel"). Sometimes, we can also use others' experiences to understand our own thoughts or behaviors. Children, for example, often make sense of their behaviors and of the surrounding environment on the basis of their caregiver's experience of the situation. These processes are often adaptive; however, in some cases, they can be disruptive. For example, if I do not really know, most of the time, how I feel or what I do think, focusing on others' thoughts and feelings may further detach me from my experience.

The cognitive/affective polarity refers to two different facets of experience. When we think about cognitive mentalizing, we refer to the understanding of the representative nature of mental states, meaning that whenever we make a statement about our own or others' behaviors or mental states (e.g. "Maria seems angry") and we are focused on cognitive mentalization, we do know that the assumption we make is only one of the infinite possible constructions on reality and that all possible constructions are true at the same time. We immediately understand how living in a world in which everything is true is quite disturbing, and this is where affective mentalization comes in handy. Affective mentalization, or mentalized affectivity, allows us to anchor the cognitive assumptions on reality to the actual affective world and is composed of three different and interdependent processes [14]: (1) identifying, (2) modulating, and (3) expressing emotions.

The internal versus external polarity refers to the focus we use for mentalizing, since we can gain the information we need to use this capacity both from the internal world ("I feel happy") or from the external world ("I am smiling"). Both these sources are reliable; however, at different times, we may tend more to the internal or external dimension for cues on how to link behaviors and mental states in a mentalized way.

The implicit (automatic) versus explicit (controlled) polarity of mentalization refers to two different processes that can operate while we mentalize. Implicit mentalization refers to implicit, fast, reflexive processes that are frequently involved in our everyday lives and allow us to navigate social interactions automatically, while explicit mentalization is the product of reflective, slow, symbolic processes that we have to use whenever automatic mentalization fails.

The authors who have developed this model of mentalization based on the aforementioned dimensions [13] have also affirmed that "these polarities mostly constitute systems in which a single representation dysfunction at one end of the pole can manifest as an excess at the other polarity. For example, a dysfunction in cognitively focused mentalization may manifest as excessively emotion-focused mental representations that (because they are not balanced by appropriate cognitive considerations) appear as inappropriate representations of emotional states" ([15], p. 20). Therefore, psychopathology may be characterized by specific patterns of imbalances in specific dimensions of mentalization, which indicate a lack of capacity on the other side of the pole. Finally, "mentalization plays an important role in affect control. Successful mentalizing is a good mediator and buffer between violent affects and the urge to act. Affect regulation is a common problem in mental problems" ([16], p. 14).

3.1 Mentalization and EDs: Trait or state?

The data on the relationship between mentalization and are sparse, and sometimes comes from research on related constructs. Martin and colleagues [17] in 2021 published a study on a sample of 176 patients with different EDs in which they used correspondence analysis to test the possible presence of specific ED subgroups. The authors found four different subgroups, characterized by different impairments and socio-demographic characteristics, and by different eating behaviors. The first group (group A) was characterized by purgative behavior, and was composed of younger patients (≤35 years old) who lived with their families and had a severe impairment. The second group (group B) was composed of individuals with different ED behaviors (purgative, restrictive and binge) who were living with their partner or children and on average older. The third group (group C) was characterized by purgative behavior and was composed of older patients (≥35 years old) who lived with their partners and children and had a less severe impairment. The fourth group (group D) was composed of individuals who tended to rely on restrictive eating behaviors, had a severe impairment, were under 35 years of age and lived with their families.

The authors examined the metacognitive capacities of each group in terms of the capacity that patients have to reflect on their inner world, operationalized as cognitive confidence but also positive beliefs about worry, self-consciousness and the need to control thoughts. Groups A and C were characterized by more severe impairments in quality of life and more severe metacognitive dysfunctions, as assessed with the Metacognition Questionnaire, thus suggesting that purgative behaviors may be related to higher impairments. Moreover, these groups were characterized by purging behaviors and different age spans (group A ≤ 35; group C ≥ 35), suggesting different processes in individuals with different ages. Moreover, different ED diagnoses were differently represented in all groups, suggesting that overcoming the categorical distinctions between specific EDs and focusing on eating behaviors and psychological processes may be useful for clinicians in their clinical practice. This result is also in line with data from a study on 100 patients with EDs, in which empathy, attachment, and different interpersonal abilities were rated [18]. The study examined the possible presence of differences between BN, AN-R, and AN-BP patients, and found only small differences between the AN-BP and BN subtypes, suggesting that these diagnostic subtypes, which refer to two distinct diagnoses, may be more similar than different.

Mentalization could also be linked to differences in the severity of symptoms. A study on a sample of ED subjects (n = 155) and healthy controls (n = 74) found, for example, that in the ED sample, those who were also self-harming had significantly more impaired mentalization [19]. In contrast to these results, however, different studies found that BN patients had mentalizing capacities that were not lower compared to healthy controls [20]. In relation to these results, Kordyńska et al. [21] have noticed that "what was observed was a significantly different distribution of the scores on the RF"[3] scale between the groups. While in the control group, close to normal distribution of the scores on RF scale was observed (with most individuals scoring in a moderate range of RF ability), in BN patients, the distribution of the RF scores was right-skewed. Scores of BN patients were also more polarized, with a greater number of individuals scoring in both low and high ranges of RF.

The authors of the study proposed that, because a much greater proportion of bulimic patients experienced childhood abuse and adversity (39% in comparison to 10% in the control group), these experiences might have forced the patients to either reflect and try to understand the behavior of their caregivers (contributing to

[3] RF stands for reflective function, the operationalization of mentalization for empirical purposes.

high scores on RF later on) or defend against reflection (low RF)" ([21], p. 28). The authors, therefore, argue that in line with the multifinality and equifinality principles of developmental psychopathology, a similar (traumatic) background may lead to different outcomes in terms of mentalization. However, there is also a further consideration related to the way mentalization is assessed and the trait/state dichotomy.

In relation to the assessment of mentalization, at the present time, not all measures are considered useful when assessing the different dimensions of mentalization considered above. Most of the measures are not able to detect and assess the specific dimensions of mentalization hypothesized in the mentalizing model and fail to encompass the multidimensionality of the construct or focus on some of the phenomenological facets of mentalizing (e.g. hyper or hypo-mentalization) (see e.g. [22]).

In addition, some studies have found that mentalization can fluctuate in different moments. Zeeck and colleagues [23] have analyzed 1232 interactions from 77 psychotherapy sessions (N = 19 ED patients; n = 6 AN-R; n = 2 AN-BP; n = 1 AN in partial remission; n = 8 BN; n = 2 OSFED) by using the in-session RF scale[4] and found that patients had overall low mentalization, and interestingly that segments in which ED symptoms were discussed were characterized by significantly lower mentalizing levels, indicating that mentalization may fluctuate in relation to the topic or issue that is the focus of attention. This result is also in line with previous studies on depression, which have shown that depressed patients tend to have lower mentalizing levels when discussing issues of loss [24].

Notwithstanding the aforementioned limitations in mentalizing assessment and the possible state fluctuations in mentalization, in 2020, Simonsen and colleagues investigated the possible presence of specific mentalizing patterns in patients with EDs [1]. Their work investigated a number of articles published before 2017 in relation to the possible presence of mentalizing profiles in EDs and found nine articles that were considered for their systematic review. The authors found that overall, ED patients tended to have lower mentalizing scores compared to healthy control, however, they noticed, "the systematic review also showed a tendency for mentalization ability about others to be more comparable between ED patients and healthy controls, indicating a mentalization profiles in patients with EDs where not all mentalization abilities are necessarily reduced to the same degree" ([1], p. 318). Therefore, a comprehensive assessment of mentalizing abilities should include an evaluation of the specific impairments related to ED pathology, the way patients can mentalize symptoms and provide a coherent and affectively attuned narrative of their disease's history.

In 2020, we conducted a study based on the same observation that Simonsen and colleagues made, in order to test the possible presence of mentalizing profiles in ED patients [25]. A sample of 157 Italian patients with different EDs (n = 44 AN-R; n = 20 AN-BP; n = 41 BN; n = 27 BED; n = 25 OSFED; 95% women[5]) completed a series of self-report measures which included a measure for the assessment of mentalization, the Reflective Functioning Questionnaire, which allows for patients to rate two of the possible phenomenological outcomes of impairments in mentalization, that is, excessive certainty about mental states and excessive uncertainty about mental states.

---

[4] The in-session RF scale provides a global score of mentalization.

[5] Please note that previous studies have found differences in mentalizing in relation to gender in adolescents [26] and the polarization of the sample on female subjects could be a source of bias in the described study.

Moreover, their clinicians completed a series of measures of mentalization, which included the Mentalization Imbalances Scale (MIS), which rates patients' imbalances on six of the dimensions of mentalization, that is, affective, cognitive, self, others, automatic and external mentalizing. Latent profile analysis was then used to test the possible presence of different mentalizing profiles in ED patients. Results indicated the presence of four different profiles:

1. ASA: affective, self and automatic imbalances.

2. E: external imbalance.

3. CSA: cognitive, self and automatic imbalances.

4. COA: cognitive, others and automatic imbalances.

The ASA profile was characterized by being excessively focused and imbalanced on the self, with difficulty in understanding others' behaviour correctly, and relying on automatic, implicit assumptions when interpreting behaviors, intentions and mental states. Moreover, there was a strong affective component, characterized by a difficulty in regulating emotions, that tends to take control over patients' actions and capacity to think clearly in situations in which emotions are particularly disturbing. This profile was also related to the most marked problematics in mentalization as self-reported by patients with the Reflective Functioning Questionnaire.

The E profile is characterized by an excessive focus on the external facets of mentalization, that is, the bodily correlates of behaviours. This profile characterizes those patients who tend to have difficulties at linking the awareness of the external facets of inner states with internal mentalization. This profile also characterizes the "less severe" patients of the considered sample.

The CSA profile is characterized by an imbalance in the cognitive facets of mentalization, with the tendency to rely on rationalization and to exclude emotions from their experiences, and to use psychotherapy as an intellectual exercise. This profile, along with the ASA profile, characterizes the most severe patients in terms of mentalization and eating pathology (number of ED criteria met by patients).

The COA profile characterizes those subjects who tend to rely on the cognitive facets of mentalization, and to exclude emotions and detach from painful or emotionally intense event, and at the same time are prone to automatic judgments and to be mostly focused on others, thus failing to reflect on their own, specific experiences and to rely on others' thoughts, feelings and behaviors to understand the world.

A subsequent study was carried out on an overall sample of 400 patients with PDs [27], and found four different mentalizing profiles, which were partially overlapping with the ones found in the previously described study on EDs. More specifically, the ASA, E, and CSA profiles were also found in patients with PDs, while the COA profile was not present. Moreover, in the PD sample, we found a profile which was labelled Others, Affective, Automatic (OAA), since it was characterized by imbalances in the others, affective and automatic facets of mentalization. Further studies on different samples and in different populations are require; however, it can be hypothesized that mentalization may play a role in the unfolding of both personality and ED symptoms, and this in turn has implications for the tailoring of interventions. Previous studies have already in fact demonstrated that improving mentalization has a role in improving interpersonal distress and problematics in mental disorders [28].

A study by Sacchetti and colleagues [29] investigated mentalizing features in a sample of 53 bulimic patients compared to healthy controls (HC) and found that bulimic patients scored lower than HC in different measures of mentalizing, which included the Reflective Functioning Questionnaire, a self-report measure, and the Reading the Mind in the Eyes Test, an experimental task[6]. The differences in the rating of mentalization were also partially explained by borderline personality features found in the bulimic patients and assessed with the Zanarini Rating Scale for Borderline Personality Disorder. Therefore, personality features are related to ED diagnosis and mentalizing problems in ED patients, and this calls for a comprehensive assessment process that includes personality and mentalization failures in the description of EDs. This is required also to provide a clinically useful description of the core features of the disorder.

4. Conclusions

This chapter tries to convey an analysis of the existing research on EDs and their relationship with mentalization and personality, in order to provide some clinically useful diagnostic tools for a population characterized by specific issues (e.g. the crossover of symptom and comorbidities) which may influence the diagnostic process.

In conclusion, this chapter has described some of the existing research on the relationship between personality and EDs and mentalization and EDs in order to provide some proposals for a clinically useful diagnosis that fully embraces all the impairments that characterize EDs and that should be targeted within treatments. It is beyond the scope of this work to provide a systematic revision of that topic. However, we have tried to highlight some of the issues that have been raised by the research. In doing so, some issues and limitations have not been discussed but deserve to be pointed out.

Some general considerations also apply to research both in relation to personality and mentalization. Although recent years' research in psychology has tried to fill this gap, the same consideration related to research in attachment applies since it "tends to refer to WEIRD individuals (Western, educated, industrialized, rich, democratic)" ([16], p. 15). Also, the majority of studies mentioned in this work are related to WEIRD subjects, therefore, its generalizability is reduced in different countries and different populations. Moreover, in relation to the ED population, it seems to be difficult to involve male subjects in research, and most studies are based on all-female or mostly female samples. Last but not least, research should focus on specific age spans, since different ages come with different challenges and problems, and research sometimes fails to acknowledge this by focusing on research samples which are representative of different generations.

This work aimed to enlighten some possible changes in the way ED diagnoses are conceptualized to provide clinically useful tools for mental health professionals. We believe that considering both personality and mentalizing characteristics and

[6] One of the problems of the assessment of mentalization is related to the use of self-report measures, which require self-reflective processes to assess reflective function, thereby generating possible conflicting processes that may cause biases in the self-reported assessment, therefore using different sources of information or experiments partially mitigates this concern.

problematics is crucial for the understanding of ED pathology, and can help tailoring interventions that foster change and may prevent symptom changes over time. A comprehensive and clinically useful assessment represents the first step toward treatment planning and a useful guide for therapists navigating the complexities of ED diagnoses.

Acknowledgements

We acknowledge the project "PROBEN 1" - grant no. PROBEN_0000011 - CUP: H53C24000540001 - "D.D. no. 1159 of 25th July 2023" under the Italian Ministry of University and Research (MUR).

Author details

Giulia Gagliardini[1*] and Antonello Colli[2]

1 Department of Humanities and Social Sciences, Meratorum University, Rome, Italy

2 Department of Humanities, Carlo Bo University of Urbino, Italy

*Address all correspondence to: giulia.gagliardini@unimercatorum.it

References

[1] Simonsen CB, Jakobsen AG, Grøntved S, Kjaersdam TG. The mentalization profile in patients with eating disorders: A systematic review and meta-analysis. Nordic Journal of Psychiatry. 2020;**74**(5):311-322. DOI: 10.1080/08039488.2019.1707869

[2] Solomon-Krakus S, Uliaszek AA, Bagby RM. Evaluating the associations between personality psychopathology and heterogeneous eating disorder behaviors: A dimensional approach. Personal Disorders. 2020;**11**(4):249-259. DOI: 10.1037/per0000358

[3] Garke M, Sörman K, Jayaram-Lindström N, Hellner C, Birgegård A. Symptom shifting and associations with mental illness: A transdiagnostic approach applied to eating disorders. Journal of Abnormal Psychology. 2019;**128**(6):585-595. DOI: 10.1037/abn0000425

[4] Robinson P, Skårderud F, Sommerfeldt B. Hunger: Mentalization-Based Treatment for Eating Disorders. Cham: Springer; 2019

[5] Barron JW. Making Diagnosis Meaningful. Enhancing Evaluation and Treatment of Psychological Disorders. New York: American Psychological Association; 1998

[6] Lindiardi V, McWilliams N, editors. Psychodynamic Diagnostic Manual. 2nd ed. New York: Guilford Press; 2017

[7] Colli A, Muzi L, Lingiardi V. A clinically useful assessment of patients' (and therapists') mental functioning: M-axis implications for the therapeutic alliance. Psychoanalytic Psychology. 2018;**35**(3):306-314. DOI: 10.1037/pap0000200

[8] Skodol AE, Oldham JM, Hyler SE, Kellman HD, Doidge N, Davies M. Comorbidity of DSM-III-R eating disorders and personality disorders. The International Journal of Eating Disorders. 1993;**14**(4):403-416. DOI: 10.1002/1098-108x(199312)14:4<403::aid-eat2260140403>3.0.co;2-x

[9] Martinussen M, Friborg O, Schmierer P, Kaiser S, Øvergård KT, Neunhoeffer AL, et al. The comorbidity of personality disorders in eating disorders: A meta-analysis. Eating and Weight Disorders. 2017;**22**(2):201-209. DOI: 10.1007/s40519-016-0345-x

[10] Westen D, Harnden-Fischer J. Personality profiles in eating disorders: Rethinking the distinction between Axis I and Axis II. American Journal of Psychiatry. 2001;**158**(4):547-562. DOI: 10.1176/appi.ajp.158.4.547

[11] Thompson-Brenner H, Westen D. Personality subtypes in eating disorders: Validation of a classification in a naturalistic sample. The British Journal of Psychiatry. 2005;**186**:516-524. DOI: 10.1192/bjp.186.6.516

[12] Gilmartin T, Gurvich C, Dipnall JF, Sharp G. One size does not fit all: Exploring how the five-factor model facets predict disordered eating behaviours among adolescent and young adult males and females. British Journal of Psychology. 2023;**114**(1):132-158. DOI: 10.1111/bjop.12601

[13] Bateman AW, Fonagy P, editors. Handbook of Mentalizing in Mental Health Practice. 2nd ed. Washington DC: American Psychiatric Association Publishing; 2019

[14] Jurist E. Minding Emotions. Cultivating Mentalization in

Psychotherapy. New York: Guilford Press; 2018

[15] Luyten P, Fonagy P, Lowyck B, Vermote R. Assessment of mentalization. In: Bateman AW, Fonagy P, editors. Handbook of Mentalizing in Mental Health Practice. Oxford: American Psychiatric Publishing; 2012. pp. 43-65

[16] Brockmann J, Kirsch H, Taubner S. Mentalizing in Psychodynamic and Psychoanalytic Psychotherapy. Basics, Applications and Case Studies. New York: Routledge; 2025

[17] Martín J, Anton-Ladislao A, Padierna Á, Berjano B, Quintana JM. Classification of subtypes of patients with eating disorders by correspondence analysis. World Journal of Psychiatry. 2021;**11**(7):375-387. DOI: 10.5498/wjp.v11.i7.375

[18] Gagliardini G, Pandolfi G, Colli A. Attachment, mentalization, emotion dysregulation, and empathy in eating disorders. The Journal of Nervous and Mental Disease. 2024;**212**:370-377. DOI: 10.1097/NMD.0000000000001781

[19] Cucchi A, Hampton JA, Moulton-Perkins A. Using the validated reflective functioning questionnaire to investigate mentalizing in individuals presenting with eating disorders with and without self-harm. PeerJ. 2018;**29**(6):e5756. DOI: 10.7717/peerj.5756

[20] Pedersen SH, Poulsen S, Lunn S. Eating disorders and mentalization: High reflective functioning in patients with bulimia nervosa. Journal of the American Psychoanalytic Association. 2015;**63**(4):671-694. DOI: 10.1177/0003065115602440

[21] Kordyńska K, Kostecka B, Kucharska K. “Walk a mile in my shoes”. Mentalising ability in patients with eating disorders – Literature review „Przejdź milę w moich butach”. Umiejętność mentalizacji u pacjentów z anoreksją i bulimią – Przegląd literatury. Neuropsychiatria i Neuropsychologia/ Neuropsychiatry and Neuropsychology. 2019;**14**(1):24-31. DOI: 10.5114/nan.2019.87728

[22] Hüwe L, Laser L, Andreas S. Observer-based and computerized measures of the patient’s mentalization in psychotherapy: A scoping review. Psychotherapy Research. 2024;**34**(4):419-433. DOI: 10.1080/10503307.2023.2226812

[23] Zeeck A, Lau I, Endorf K, Schaefer L, Euler S, Lahmann C, et al. Mentalizing in psychotherapeutic processes of patients with eating disorders. Frontiers in Psychiatry. 2024;**15**:1367863. DOI: 10.3389/fpsyt.2024.1367863

[24] Taubner S, Kessler H, Buchheim A, Kächele H, Staun L. The role of mentalization in the psychoanalytic treatment of chronic depression. Psychiatry. 2011;**74**(1):49-57. DOI: 10.1521/psyc.2011.74.1.49

[25] Gagliardini G, Gullo S, Tinozzi V, Baiano M, Balestrieri M, Todisco P, et al. Mentalizing subtypes in eating disorders: A latent profile analysis. Frontiers in Psychology. 2020;**11**:564291. DOI: 10.3389/fpsyg.2020.564291

[26] Poznyak E, Morosan L, Perroud N, Speranza M, Badoud D, Debbané M. Roles of age, gender and psychological difficulties in adolescent mentalizing. Journal of Adolescence. 2019;**74**:120-129. DOI: 10.1016/j.adolescence.2019.06.007

[27] Gagliardini G, Gullo S, Teti A, Colli A. Personality and mentalization: A latent profile analysis of mentalizing problematics in adult patients. Journal of Clinical Psychology. 2023;**79**:514-530. DOI: 10.1002/jclp.23430

[28] Hayden MC, Müllauer PK, Gaugeler R, Senft B, Andreas S. Improvements in mentalization predict improvements in interpersonal distress in patients with mental disorders. Journal of Clinical Psychology. 2018;**74**(12):2276-2286. DOI: 10.1002/jclp.22673

[29] Sacchetti S, Robinson P, Bogaardt A, Clare A, Ouellet-Courtois C, Luyten P, et al. Reduced mentalizing in patients with bulimia nervosa and features of borderline personality disorder: A case-control study. BMC Psychiatry. 2019;**19**:134. DOI: 10.1186/s12888-019-2112-9

Chapter 6

The Effect of Bariatric Surgery on Eating Disorders

Hatice Toprak and Şükrü Salih Toprak

Abstract

Eating disorders are associated with many factors such as addictions, psychological conditions, food insecurity, personality traits, and educational status. Obesity and eating disorders are common clinical conditions. Bariatric surgery is the most effective treatment method for obesity. It is common for eating disorders to be more common in individuals who have undergone bariatric surgery. Therefore, individuals who undergo bariatric surgery for eating disorder research represent a unique population. It was proven in many studies that bariatric surgeries contribute to the remission of physical comorbidities in individuals with obesity. However, its effect on eating disorders has not yet been fully explained. Restrictive bariatric procedures may have an inherently positive impact on eating disorders. Limited data are available on long-term follow-up results. The relationship between surgical failure rates and eating disorders in the post-bariatric period is among the other topics of interest. In this section, eating disorders seen in individuals undergoing bariatric surgery and the success of bariatric surgery in individuals with eating disorders will be discussed.

Keywords: bariatric surgery, post-bariatric period, surgical failure rates, common clinical conditions, food insecurity

1. Introduction

Eating disorders (ED) are complex psychiatric conditions with an increasing prevalence and are associated with psychological and physical disorders that attract the attention of clinicians [1]. If not treated promptly, EDs are severe and often chronic [1]. Individuals with ED are at risk for poorer quality of life [2]. Binge eating disorder (BED) is associated with obesity, and those seeking help for BED often present with weight-related referrals [3]. The incidence of BED is common in populations seeking weight loss treatment and particularly among candidates for bariatric surgery (BS) [4]. The parallel relationship between obesity and COVID-19 violence [5] has increased the importance of tackling obesity in countries' health systems. The fight against obesity is valuable in identifying the precursors of obesity. BED can be seen as the premise of obesity.

Obesity is a global healthcare concern. BS is the most effective and permanent treatment modality for obesity. The most frequently performed bariatric procedure is Sleeve Gastrectomy (SG), and Roux-en-Y gastric bypass (RYGB) is the second most frequently performed operation in this respect. Revisional BSs are performed with a frequency of 7% among all bariatric procedures. Body mass index (BMI) is the most appropriate and frequently employed criterion for BSs. The accepted surgical body mass index (BMI) threshold value for BSs is BMI ≥ 40 kg/m^2, and BMI ≥ 35 kg/m^2 in the presence of additional medical problems. BMI is a value independent of age, gender, ethnicity, and body fat distribution differences. The success of BSs varies between individuals and according to the types of surgical procedures. Perioperative mortality for BSs varies between 0.03% and 2% [6–8]. Individuals with obesity must be kept under lifelong medical supervision after BS [9].

2. Definition of eating disorders and their frequency in society

The most recognized eating disorders are Anorexia Nervosa (AN), Bulimia Nervosa (BN), and BED [10]. AN and BN eating disorders are characterized by excessive weight control behaviors with a thin ideal. What they have in common is a very strong concern about body image. People are underweight and engage in various behaviors to prevent weight gain in Anorexia Nervosa. People with Bulimia Nervosa are not underweight. They engage in a cycle of binge eating, vomiting, and/or fasting/compulsive exercise [11]. BED can be defined as a clinical condition characterized by binge eating, in which individuals lose control of their eating behaviors, and consume larger amounts of food when compared to other individuals. The first known definition was made by Stunkard in 1959 in this respect [12]. Contrary to BN, binge eating episodes are not regularly followed by inappropriate compensatory behaviors aimed at preventing weight gain (self-induced vomiting, off-label use of laxatives or enemas, strenuous exercises, etc.) [13]. It has an estimated incidence between 0.3% and 1.8%, with a complex etiology that may be associated with environmental and genetic factors. BED occurs in 2.8% (0.6–5.8%) of women and 1.0% (0.3–2.0%) of men. Objective binge eating (OBE) is defined as the consumption of objectively large amounts of food accompanied by loss of control (LOC). The presence of LOC must be identified for a definitive diagnosis of BED [14]. Rapid and uncomfortable eating to satiety, eating alone because of embarrassment, is considered in patients with BED [15]. There are very few studies conducted previously on the prevalence of eating disorders in the general population [11, 13, 16].

Measures implemented during the COVID-19 pandemic, including house arrest, affected the living habits of individuals [17]. An increase in the number of ED individuals diagnosed during the COVID-19 pandemic was observed [18]. The COVID-19 pandemic is considered to have increased the risk and symptoms of eating disorders (ED) [19]. Higher education levels, body image-related factors, and appearance-focused social media use are also considered to be associated with an increased risk of eating disorder symptoms [1].

3. Eating disorders and mood

Extreme obesity is associated with a significant psychosocial burden, including decreased quality of life, body image concerns, sexual behaviors, and impairments in other areas of psychosocial functioning [20]. Mental health conditions such as depression and binge eating disorders, as well as substance abuse, are detected at higher rates among MBS candidates compared to the general population [8]. The concept of "food addiction" is based on the criteria for Substance Use Disorder and is common in individuals with BED as a diagnostic reality and can be detected in individuals without mental illness and the general population [21]. It was speculated that the underlying brain mechanisms are similar to those that ultimately cause compulsive drug consumption in addiction [22]. There are similarities between BED and substance addictions, including craving for the desired substance, a sense of loss of control, repetitive attempts to control use, and a large amount of time spent obtaining or using the substance.

Another psychiatric condition that researchers have recently focused on in adults undergoing obesity treatment is attention deficit hyperactivity disorder (ADHD). In their study, Altfas et al. reported that ADHD was quite common in individuals with obesity. This prevalence was most significant in individuals with a BMI > 40 [23].

4. Obesity and structural brain anomalies

Some structural brain anomalies were described in studies conducted with obese individuals [24]. Raji et al. compared obese elderly individuals with BMI > 30 and normal-weight elderly individuals with BMI < 18.5 < 25 in their study and reported atrophy in the frontal lobes, anterior cingulate gyrus, hippocampus, and thalamus [25]. The study associated high BMI with lower brain volume. Yokum et al. reported lower gray matter and white matter volumes in the brains of young women who had obesity [26]. The relationship between structural brain anomalies in obese individuals and eating habits was examined in various studies. Decreased basal metabolism and dopaminergic changes in the prefrontal cortex and striatum in obese individuals are associated with increased activation of reward brain regions in response to palatable food cues. Increased reward region response might increase food desire and trigger weight gain [27]. It was presented in several studies that BS may also promote the recovery of obesity-related brain functional and structural abnormalities [24, 28, 29].

Executive function performance may be decreased in individuals who have obesity. Deficits in working memory, mental flexibility, motor speed, and complex attention might also be detected [30, 31].

5. Diagnosis and treatment of eating disorders

There might be delays in clinicians' diagnosis of ED patients due to various reasons. Some of the reasons that prevent individuals with ED from seeking help for treatment are stigmatization and shame, denial of the illness, treatment costs, lack of information, and lack of social support [32]. A study conducted on ED patients reported that there was an average delay of 5.28 years between the onset of ED symptoms and seeking treatment [33]. It is important to provide basic training to increase clinicians' awareness of ED. Evidence-based specific psychological and pharmacological treatments are recommended for most eating disorders [34]. The literature reports that standard weight loss treatments, including BS, do not worsen the eating habits of individuals with ED. Eating disorders and obesity treatments appear to be beneficial in BED [3]. BED is the second most common psychiatric disorder in the bariatric surgery population after major depressive disorder. Considering the increased number of individuals with obesity, psychiatric evaluations before BS might increase the success of surgery [35].

6. Effects of bariatric surgery on eating disorders

BS is gaining attention for its effectiveness when compared to behavioral and pharmacological interventions in combating obesity and eating disorders. Various studies report BED rates ranging from 6–64% in individuals undergoing BS [10, 36]. In general, the initial treatment approach in these patients is directed at the eating disorder-associated psychopathology [37]. Bariatric surgery is indicated for patients with clinically severe obesity [37].

It is expected that surgical failure, mortality, and morbidity rates associated with BS will decrease with developing laparoscopic techniques and increasing surgical experience. BSs include different procedures with restrictive [e.g., sleeve gastrectomy (SG), malabsorptive (biliopancreatic diversion)], or mixed [Roux-en-Y gastric bypass (RYGB)] effects [14]. BSs include interventions that change the amount of food that patients can eat, changing the physiological capacity of swallowing and digestion significantly [14]. Also, different procedures might change the patient's diet, eating habits, and weight loss status over various processes. For example, the stomach size is decreased to reduce calorie intake in SG and the decreased calorie intake after the surgery is the first driving force of weight loss [38]. Effective weight loss was recorded after Gastric Bypass (GB) surgery [39]. However, patients who were depressed and had binge eating problems who underwent GB surgery were associated with less weight loss [40].

The increased psychosocial burden of individuals is an important reason for the decision to have BS [31]. Improvements in psychosocial status and functionality are reported following surgery in obese individuals who have had BS. In obese individuals, depressive symptoms were reported to improve significantly within a two-year follow-up period following BS, but the risk of suicide and self-harm was reported to increase [41]. Impulse control is an important factor in eating behaviors and extreme obesity and might cause less weight loss than expected after BS and psychosocial distress ([31], p. 20). Previous studies associated BS with less weight loss in patients with eating disorders [3, 40, 42, 43]. In their study, Chao et al. reported that patients with BED diagnosis who underwent surgery 2 years after Roux-en-Y Gastric Bypass (RYGB) and Laparoscopic Adjustable Gastric Banding (LAGB) lost 18.6% of their preoperative initial weight, compared to 23.9% in patients without BED [44]. In their observational cohort study, Lüscher et al. concluded that individuals with ED regained weight after BS by 2.4% when compared to patients without ED. This difference was not statistically significant [45].

7. Problems with BS

BS offers significant improvements in mortality and morbidity in individuals with obesity [46]. Defined as failure to lose 40–60% of initial excess body weight (EWL) within 1–2 years, inadequate weight loss occurs with a frequency of 11–22% in individuals undergoing BS [47]. Inadequate weight loss might be influenced by many conditions following BS. Psychosocial predictors were also identified in several studies [48]. Failure to achieve significant weight loss following bariatric surgery is likely multifactorial and might involve several patient-level characteristics. Psychosocial and behavioral predictors that might be associated with the degree of weight loss were identified. Inappropriate eating habits [40, 49], exercise and mobility restrictions [50], postoperative support [51], and failure to participate in follow-up programs [52] were implicated predictors in this regard.

Weight regain is another issue in long-term follow-ups. There is no clarity about the prevalence, criterion, and timing of weight regain after BS. King et al. reported that a weight gain of ≥20 from the maximum weight loss (%MWL) was associated with decreased quality of life, decreased satisfaction, and worsening medical comorbidities such as diabetes and hypertension [53]. In another study that examined the 7-year follow-up results of 300 patients after RYGB, 37% of the patients suffered from weight regain [54]. Weight regain develops after the lowest weight following GB, but the mortality rate remains low at 3.1% [55]. In another study, this rate was reported to be 76% for SG at 6-year follow-up [56]. It was reported in a meta-analysis that the length of follow-up, anatomic and genetic predisposition, and dietary and psychiatric factors might also be associated with weight regain [57]. The gastrojejunal stoma diameter and excess stomach volume associated with the surgical procedure were presented as anatomical factors in previous studies [58, 59]. Regarding hormonal factors, Santo et al. found that elevated initial leptin levels and increased postoperative glucose-dependent insulinotropic polypeptide (GIP) and glucagon-like peptide 1 (GLP-1) secretion were associated with weight regain [60]. Masha et al. reported significant relationships between low physical activity, low self-esteem, eating disorders, and weight regain in their study that was conducted to determine behavioral predictors of weight regain in patients following GB [48]. Christou et al. followed morbidly obese (BMI < 50 kg/m^2) and super obese (BMI > 50 kg/m^2) patients for 10 years and found the failure rate to be 20.4% in morbidly obese patients and 34.9% in super obese patients [55].

The effectiveness of psychosocial interventions following BS is also of interest to researchers. A previous study investigated the effectiveness of telephone-based cognitive behavioral therapy 1 year after BS and reported that it did not cause any change in short-term weight outcomes but improved disordered eating and psychological distress [61]. These results in the literature show that it is important to identify high-risk patients for an eating disorder diagnosis, to follow-up postoperatively, and to develop additional interventions if these behaviors continue in the postoperative period [62]. Weight regain is an undesirable situation for BS patients, and it is necessary to develop psychosocial interventions that prevent weight gain [47, 53, 61].

Methods to increase the success of bariatric surgery are a subject that is being evaluated by researchers. It has been presented in the literature that cognitive and behavioral therapies improve post-BS outcomes in individuals undergoing BS [63]. Cognitive and behavioral therapy can increase the success of BS both medically and psychologically [64]. Therapies can be applied face-to-face or *via* telephone and internet-mediated technologies. The effectiveness of telephone-mediated therapies on depression and obsessive-compulsive disorder has been evaluated in previous studies. Positive results were reported for both psychological problems [65, 66]. There is no consensus on whether it should be applied before or after BS. In one study, it was reported that therapies to be applied after BS may be more effective [67]. Long-term follow-up data on cognitive and behavioral therapies discussed for inclusion in BS care programs are needed.

8. Conclusion

The frequency of ED in patients presenting for BS is at considerable levels. Individuals who have ED benefit from obesity treatments including BS. Weight regain associated with failure for BS is more significant in individuals with BED. Meticulous psychiatric evaluations before BS are important for planning postoperative interventions. Individuals with obesity and their guardians must be informed about this risk during preoperative evaluations before BS. Long-term follow-up of individuals with BS must be performed. Possible problems associated with eating habits must be identified, and additional interventions, primarily postoperative supportive treatments, must be planned.

Author details

Hatice Toprak[1*] and Şükrü Salih Toprak[2]

1 Department of Anesthesiology and Reanimation, Karamanoğlu Mehmetbey University, Karaman, Turkey

2 Department of General Surgery, Karamanoğlu Mehmetbey University, Karaman, Turkey

*Address all correspondence to: dr.tprk@hotmail.com

References

[1] Barakat S et al. Risk factors for eating disorders: Findings from a rapid review. Journal of Eating Disorders. 2023;**11**:8. DOI: 10.1186/s40337-022-00717-4

[2] Jenkins PE, Hoste RR, Meyer C, Blissett JM. Eating disorders and quality of life: A review of the literature. Clinical Psychology Review. 2011;**31**(1):113-121. DOI: 10.1016/j.cpr.2010.08.003

[3] de Zwaan M et al. Characteristics of morbidly obese patients before gastric bypass surgery. Comprehensive Psychiatry. 2003;**44**(5):428-434. DOI: 10.1016/S0010-440X(03)00092-0

[4] Mitchell JE et al. Eating behavior and eating disorders in adults before bariatric surgery. The International Journal of Eating Disorders. 2015;**48**(2):215-222. DOI: 10.1002/eat.22275

[5] de, Leeuw AJ, Oude Luttikhuis MA, Wellen AC, Müller C, Calkhoven CF. Obesity and its impact on COVID-19. Journal of Molecular Medicine. 2021;**99**(7). DOI: 10.1007/s00109-021-02072-4

[6] Angrisani L, Santonicola A, Iovino P, Ramos A, Shikora S, Kow L. Bariatric surgery survey 2018: Similarities and disparities among the 5 IFSO chapters. Obesity Surgery. 2021;**31**(5):1937-1948. DOI: 10.1007/s11695-020-05207-7

[7] Arterburn DE, Telem DA, Kushner RF, Courcoulas AP. Benefits and risks of bariatric surgery in adults: A review. JAMA. 2020;**324**(9):879-887. DOI: 10.1001/jama.2020.12567

[8] Eisenberg D et al. 2022 American Society for Metabolic and Bariatric Surgery (ASMBS) and International Federation for the Surgery of obesity and metabolic disorders (IFSO): Indications for metabolic and bariatric surgery. Surgery for Obesity and Related Diseases. 2022;**0**(0). DOI: 10.1016/j.soard.2022.08.013

[9] Consensus Development Conference Panel. Gastrointestinal surgery for severe obesity. Annals of Internal Medicine. 1991;**115**(12):956-961. DOI: 10.7326/0003-4819-115-12-956

[10] D'Souza C, Hay P, Touyz S, Piya MK. Bariatric and cosmetic surgery in people with eating disorders. Nutrients. 2020;**12**(9):2861. DOI: 10.3390/nu12092861

[11] Hay P. Current approach to eating disorders: A clinical update. Internal Medicine Journal. 2020;**50**(1):24-29. DOI: 10.1111/imj.14691

[12] Stunkard AJ. Eating patterns and obesity. The Psychiatric Quarterly. 1959;**33**(2):284-295. DOI: 10.1007/BF01575455

[13] Giel KE et al. Binge eating disorder. Nature Reviews. Disease Primers. 2022;**8**(1):16. DOI: 10.1038/s41572-022-00344-y

[14] Conceição EM, Utzinger LM, Pisetsky EM. Eating disorders and problematic eating behaviours before and after bariatric surgery: Characterization, assessment and association with treatment outcomes. European Eating Disorders Review. 2015;**23**(6):417-425. DOI: 10.1002/erv.2397

[15] Aylward L, Konsor M, Cox S. Binge eating before and after bariatric surgery. Current Obesity Reports. 2022;**11**(4):386-394. DOI: 10.1007/s13679-022-00486-w

[16] Hay P, Mitchison D, Collado AEL, González-Chica DA, Stocks N, Touyz S. Burden and health-related quality of life of eating disorders, including avoidant/restrictive food intake disorder (ARFID), in the Australian population. Journal of Eating Disorders. 2017;**5**:21. DOI: 10.1186/s40337-017-0149-z

[17] Ammar A et al. Effects of COVID-19 home confinement on eating behaviour and physical activity: Results of the ECLB-COVID19 international online survey. Nutrients. 2020;**12**(6) Art. no. 6. DOI: 10.3390/nu12061583

[18] Devoe DJ et al. The impact of the COVID-19 pandemic on eating disorders: A systematic review. The International Journal of Eating Disorders. 2022:10. 1002/eat.23704. DOI: 10.1002/eat.23704

[19] Rodgers RF et al. The impact of the COVID-19 pandemic on eating disorder risk and symptoms. The International Journal of Eating Disorders. 2020;**53**(7): 1166-1170. DOI: 10.1002/eat.23318

[20] Sarwer DB, Lavery M, Spitzer JC. A review of the relationships between extreme obesity, quality of life, and sexual function. Obesity Surgery. 2012;**22**(4):668-676. DOI: 10.1007/s11695-012-0588-1

[21] di Giacomo E et al. Disentangling binge eating disorder and food addiction: A systematic review and meta-analysis. Eating and Weight Disorders. 2022;**27**(6):1963-1970. DOI: 10.1007/s40519-021-01354-7

[22] Volkow ND, Wise RA. How can drug addiction help us understand obesity? Nature Neuroscience. 2005;**8**(5):555-560. DOI: 10.1038/nn1452

[23] Altfas JR. Prevalence of attention deficit/hyperactivity disorder among adults in obesity treatment. BMC Psychiatry. 2002;**2**:9. DOI: 10.1186/1471-244x-2-9

[24] Hu Y et al. Brain connectivity, and hormonal and Behavioral correlates of sustained weight loss in obese patients after laparoscopic sleeve gastrectomy. Cerebral Cortex. 2021;**31**(2):1284-1295. DOI: 10.1093/cercor/bhaa294

[25] Raji CA et al. Brain structure and obesity. Human Brain Mapping. 2010;**31**(3):353-364. DOI: 10.1002/hbm.20870

[26] Yokum S, Ng J, Stice E. Relation of regional gray and white matter volumes to current BMI and future increases in BMI: A prospective MRI study. International Journal of Obesity. 2005, 2012;**36**(5):656-664. DOI: 10.1038/ijo.2011.175

[27] Val-Laillet D et al. Neuroimaging and neuromodulation approaches to study eating behavior and prevent and treat eating disorders and obesity. NeuroImage: Clinical. 2015;**8**:1-31. DOI: 10.1016/j.nicl.2015.03.016

[28] Li G et al. Brain functional and structural magnetic resonance imaging of obesity and weight loss interventions. Molecular Psychiatry. 2023;**28**(4):1466-1479. DOI: 10.1038/s41380-023-02025-y

[29] Zhang Y et al. Ghrelin reductions following bariatric surgery were associated with decreased resting state activity in the hippocampus. International Journal of Obesity. 2019;**43**(4):842-851. DOI: 10.1038/s41366-018-0126-x

[30] Gunstad J, Paul RH, Cohen RA, Tate DF, Spitznagel MB, Gordon E. Elevated body mass index is associated with executive dysfunction in otherwise healthy adults. Comprehensive

Psychiatry. 2007;**48**(1):57-61. DOI: 10.1016/j.comppsych.2006.05.001

[31] Sarwer DB et al. Psychopathology, disordered eating, and impulsivity as predictors of outcomes of bariatric surgery. Surgery for Obesity and Related Diseases: The Official Journal of the American Society for Metabolic and Bariatric Surgery. 2019;**15**(4):650-655. DOI: 10.1016/j.soard.2019.01.029

[32] Ali K, Farrer L, Fassnacht DB, Gulliver A, Bauer S, Griffiths KM. Perceived barriers and facilitators towards help-seeking for eating disorders: A systematic review. The International Journal of Eating Disorders. 2017;**50**(1):9-21. DOI: 10.1002/eat.22598

[33] Hamilton A et al. Understanding treatment delay: Perceived barriers preventing treatment-seeking for eating disorders. The Australian and New Zealand Journal of Psychiatry. 2022;**56**(3):248-259. DOI: 10.1177/00048674211020102

[34] Hay P et al. Royal Australian and new Zealand College of Psychiatrists clinical practice guidelines for the treatment of eating disorders. The Australian and New Zealand Journal of Psychiatry. 2014;**48**(11):977-1008. DOI: 10.1177/0004867414555814

[35] Sarwer DB et al. Psychiatric diagnoses and psychiatric treatment among bariatric surgery candidates. Obesity Surgery. 2004;**14**(9):1148-1156. DOI: 10.1381/0960892042386922

[36] Niego SH, Kofman MD, Weiss JJ, Geliebter A. Binge eating in the bariatric surgery population: A review of the literature. The International Journal of Eating Disorders. 2007;**40**(4):349-359. DOI: 10.1002/eat.20376

[37] Mechanick JI et al. Clinical practice guidelines for the perioperative nutritional, metabolic, and nonsurgical support of the bariatric surgery patient--2013 update: Cosponsored by American Association of Clinical Endocrinologists, the Obesity Society, and American Society for Metabolic and Bariatric Surgery. Endocrine Practice: Official Journal of the American College of Endocrinology and the American Association of Clinical Endocrinologists. 2013;**19**(2):337-372. DOI: 10.4158/EP12437.GL

[38] Diamantis T, Apostolou KG, Alexandrou A, Griniatsos J, Felekouras E, Tsigris C. Review of long-term weight loss results after laparoscopic sleeve gastrectomy. Surgery for Obesity and Related Diseases: The Official Journal of the American Society for Metabolic and Bariatric Surgery. 2014;**10**(1):177-183. DOI: 10.1016/j.soard.2013.11.007

[39] Perugini RA et al. Predictors of complication and suboptimal weight loss after laparoscopic roux-en-Y gastric bypass: A series of 188 patients. Archives of surgery (Chicago, Ill.: 1960). 2003;**138**(5):541-545; discussion 545-546. DOI: 10.1001/archsurg.138.5.541

[40] Toussi R, Fujioka K, Coleman KJ. Pre- and Postsurgery Behavioral compliance, patient health, and Postbariatric surgical weight loss. Obesity. 2009;**17**(5):996-1002. DOI: 10.1038/oby.2008.628

[41] Law S, Dong S, Zhou F, Zheng D, Wang C, Dong Z. Bariatric surgery and mental health outcomes: An umbrella review. Frontiers in Endocrinology. 2023;**14**:1283621. DOI: 10.3389/fendo.2023.1283621

[42] Guisado Macias JA, Vaz Leal FJ. Psychopathological differences between morbidly obese binge eaters and non-binge eaters after bariatric surgery. Eating and Weight Disorders - Studies on Anorexia, Bulimia and Obesity.

2003;**8**(4):315-318. DOI: 10.1007/BF03325032

[43] Hsu LKG et al. Nonsurgical factors that influence the outcome of bariatric surgery: A review. Biopsychosocial Science and Medicine. 1998;**60**(3):338

[44] Chao AM et al. Binge-eating disorder and the outcome of bariatric surgery in a prospective, observational study: Two-year results. Obesity. 2016;**24**(11):2327-2333. DOI: 10.1002/oby.21648

[45] Lüscher A et al. Impact of preoperative psychiatric profile in bariatric surgery on long-term weight outcome. Obesity Surgery. 2023;**33**(7):2072-2082. DOI: 10.1007/s11695-023-06595-2

[46] Arterburn DE et al. Association between bariatric surgery and long-term survival. JAMA. 2015;**313**(1):62-70. DOI: 10.1001/jama.2014.16968

[47] Noria SF, Shelby RD, Atkins KD, Nguyen NT, Gadde KM. Weight regain after bariatric surgery: Scope of the problem, causes, prevention, and treatment. Current Diabetes Reports. 2023;**23**(3):31-42. DOI: 10.1007/s11892-023-01498-z

[48] Livhits M et al. Patient behaviors associated with weight regain after laparoscopic gastric bypass. Obesity Research & Clinical Practice. 2011;**5**(3):e258-e265. DOI: 10.1016/j.orcp.2011.03.004

[49] Sarwer DB et al. Preoperative eating behavior, postoperative dietary adherence, and weight loss after gastric bypass surgery. Surgery for Obesity and Related Diseases. 2008;**4**(5):640-646. DOI: 10.1016/j.soard.2008.04.013

[50] Bond DS et al. Impact of self-reported physical activity participation on proportion of excess weight loss and BMI among gastric bypass surgery patients. The American Surgeon. 2004;**70**(9):811-814. DOI: 10.1177/000313480407000913

[51] Orth WS, Madan AK, Taddeucci RJ, Coday M, Tichansky DS. Support group meeting attendance is associated with better weight loss. Obesity Surgery. 2008;**18**(4):391-394. DOI: 10.1007/s11695-008-9444-8

[52] Gould JC, Beverstein G, Reinhardt S, Garren MJ. Impact of routine and long-term follow-up on weight loss after laparoscopic gastric bypass. Surgery for Obesity and Related Diseases. 2007;**3**(6):627-630. DOI: 10.1016/j.soard.2007.07.005

[53] King WC, Hinerman AS, Belle SH, Wahed AS, Courcoulas AP. Comparison of the performance of common measures of weight regain after bariatric surgery for association with clinical outcomes. JAMA. 2018;**320**(15):1560-1569. DOI: 10.1001/jama.2018.14433

[54] Cooper TC, Simmons EB, Webb K, Burns JL, Kushner RF. Trends in weight regain following roux-en-Y gastric bypass (RYGB) bariatric surgery. Obesity Surgery. 2015;**25**(8):1474-1481. DOI: 10.1007/s11695-014-1560-z

[55] Christou NV, Look D, MacLean LD. Weight gain after short- and long-limb gastric bypass in patients followed for longer than 10 years. Annals of Surgery. 2006;**244**(5):734-740. DOI: 10.1097/01.sla.0000217592.04061.d5

[56] Lauti M, Kularatna M, Hill AG, MacCormick AD. Weight regain following sleeve gastrectomy—A systematic review. Obesity Surgery. 2016;**26**(6):1326-1334. DOI: 10.1007/s11695-016-2152-x

[57] Athanasiadis DI, Martin A, Kapsampelis P, Monfared S, Stefanidis D. Factors associated with weight regain post-bariatric surgery: A systematic review. Surgical Endoscopy. 2021;**35**(8):4069-4084. DOI: 10.1007/s00464-021-08329-w

[58] Dayyeh BKA, Lautz DB, Thompson CC. Gastrojejunal stoma diameter predicts weight regain after roux-en-Y gastric bypass. Clinical Gastroenterology and Hepatology. 2011;**9**(3):228-233. DOI: 10.1016/j.cgh.2010.11.004

[59] Alvarez V et al. Mechanisms of long-term weight regain in patients undergoing sleeve gastrectomy. Nutrition. 2016;**32**(3):303-308. DOI: 10.1016/j.nut.2015.08.023

[60] Santo MA et al. Weight regain after gastric bypass: Influence of gut hormones. Obesity Surgery. 2016;**26**(5):919-925. DOI: 10.1007/s11695-015-1908-z

[61] Sockalingam S et al. Efficacy of telephone-based cognitive Behavioral therapy for weight loss, disordered eating, and psychological distress after bariatric surgery: A randomized clinical trial. JAMA Network Open. 2023;**6**(8):e2327099. DOI: 10.1001/jamanetworkopen.2023.27099

[62] Meany G, Conceição E, Mitchell JE. Binge eating, binge eating disorder and loss of control eating: Effects on weight outcomes after bariatric surgery. European Eating Disorders Review. 2014;**22**(2):87-91. DOI: 10.1002/erv.2273

[63] Rudolph A, Hilbert A. Post-operative behavioural management in bariatric surgery: A systematic review and meta-analysis of randomized controlled trials. Obesity Reviews. 2013;**14**(4):292-302. DOI: 10.1111/obr.12013

[64] Cheroutre C, Guerrien A, Rousseau A. Contributing of cognitive-Behavioral therapy in the context of bariatric surgery: A review of the literature. Obesity Surgery. 2020;**30**(8):3154-3166. DOI: 10.1007/s11695-020-04627-9

[65] Mohr DC et al. Telephone-administered psychotherapy for depression. Archives of General Psychiatry. 2005;**62**(9):1007-1014. DOI: 10.1001/archpsyc.62.9.1007

[66] Lovell K et al. Telephone administered cognitive behaviour therapy for treatment of obsessive compulsive disorder: Randomised controlled non-inferiority trial. BMJ. 2006;**333**(7574):883. DOI: 10.1136/bmj.38940.355602.80

[67] Conceição EM, Goldschmidt A. Disordered eating after bariatric surgery: Clinical aspects, impact on outcomes, and intervention strategies. Current Opinion in Psychiatry. 2019;**32**(6):504. DOI: 10.1097/YCO.0000000000000549

Chapter 7

Obesity and Eating Disorders: A Balance of Interventions

Iakovina Koutoufa

Abstract

Eating disorders and obesity are part of a common spectrum, and their comorbidity is increasing, leading to increased challenges in balancing often opposing treatments. This chapter reviews some of the evidence around shared and distinctive etiological pathways of eating disorders and obesity and how they are addressed in treatment while focusing on two primary areas where the two conditions interact: body image and eating behaviors. With regards to body image, this chapter explores body dissatisfaction in eating disorders and obesity, as well as the impact of weight stigma. The impact of eating behaviors and dieting are also examined as well as the benefits of weight loss in managing physical conditions associated with obesity. Lastly, this chapter summarizes the implications of comorbidity between obesity and eating disorders on pharmacological and psychological treatment approaches in relation to managing weight loss, weight stigma, and body image and makes recommendations for best practice when treating individuals who present with both.

Keywords: eating disorders, obesity, weight management, weight loss, body image, dieting, weight stigma, binge eating disorder

1. Introduction

There is accumulating evidence of the strong association between obesity and eating disorders. Both conditions share psychological, sociocultural, and medical characteristics but also differ importantly in others. Both are crucial for healthcare professionals to understand in order to deliver effective, personalized care without causing harm. One of the greatest controversies in treating individuals with both obesity and eating disorders is ensuring that treatment plans address both physical health and psychological well-being without exacerbating one condition by treating the other. In obesity treatments, the focus is primarily on weight loss with the aim of reducing the risk of further health complications. In eating disorder treatments, the focus is shifted *away* from weight loss, and the power of weight as a measurement of progress is challenged. This controversy presents a real challenge when obesity and eating disorders co-occur in the same individual.

Eating disorders (EDs) are mental health conditions characterized by persistent and unhelpful eating habits such as restrictive dieting, excessive eating, or disordered behaviors around the consumption and absorption of food associated with distress and dysfunction. More specifically, the most common eating disorders are anorexia nervosa, bulimia nervosa, binge eating disorder, and other specified feeding or eating disorder. Anorexia nervosa (AN) is characterized by nutritional restriction associated with significantly low body weight, persistent disturbance in one's perception of their body weight or shape, and intense fear of weight gain associated with behaviors that disturb weight gain. On the other hand, bulimia nervosa (BN) is characterized by episodes of binge eating (i.e., eating large amounts of food within any 2-hour period with a sense of lack of control) that are often followed by recurrent compensatory behaviors to prevent weight gain (e.g., purging, misuse of laxatives or diuretics, fasting, or excessive exercise). Individuals with BN tend to evaluate themselves unduly based on their body weight and shape. Binge eating disorder (BED) is characterized by binge-eating episodes; however, there is an absence of compensatory behaviors, and it is often accompanied either by rapid pace of eating, eating until uncomfortably full, eating large amounts of food when not feeling physically hungry, eating in secret, or feeling disgusted with oneself or guilty after overeating. Individuals that do not fully meet the above criteria are diagnosed with other specified feeding or eating disorder (OSFED) [1].

Eating disorders were historically conceptualized as disorders in people with low weight. It was not until the 1980s with the introduction of the DSM-III where BN was first introduced as a separate diagnostic category [2]. There is now overwhelming evidence that EDs are not detected solely in people with low weight. In fact, some of the most common EDs are identified in a large range of body types and weights. The World Health Organization (WHO) Mental Health Survey Initiative found that approximately 40% of respondents with BN or BED also had obesity in the past year [3]. In populations seeking treatment for obesity, a percentage ranging from 9% to 29% meets the diagnostic criteria for BED. In individuals with a body mass index (BMI) over 50 seeking bariatric surgery, BED can be identified in up to 50% of cases [4]. A study of a large sample in the Italian adult population with obesity identified that 12% of individuals with obesity also presented with BED, which is higher than the average incidence of BED (3%) within the overall adult Italian population [5]. Similarly, in Latin America, it was found that BED was prevalent in a percentage of 16–52% in populations with obesity [6]. In the United States, participants in a large sample who met criteria for BED at some point in their lives were more likely to struggle with obesity compared to individuals who had no history of EDs [7].

Obesity is a condition characterized by a BMI of 30 kg/m^2 or higher as a measure of adiposity. In 2022, 1 in 8 people in the world were living with obesity. Worldwide adult obesity has more than doubled since 1990, and adolescent obesity has quadrupled [8]. Obesity is strongly associated with multiple health conditions such as diabetes mellitus, musculoskeletal and respiratory problems, cardiovascular disease, certain cancers, and higher mortality rates [9–12]. Given the multiple complications associated with obesity and the cost it presents in healthcare services, there is an imperative priority to develop policies that prevent and treat obesity by addressing the multitude of aspects that contribute to its onset and maintenance.

While both EDs and obesity carry such physical and psychological risks, it is important to examine carefully the individual constellations of symptoms in each affected individual. Not everyone with obesity will have an ED, and not everyone with an ED will have obesity. One important distinction is that individuals with EDs tend to exhibit dysfunctional attitudes and beliefs toward food, associated with guilt, fear, and shame [13], whereas individuals with obesity do not necessarily portray these attitudes and beliefs [14]. It is important to highlight that there is significant bias associating obesity and EDs, often fueled by social prejudice and the simplistic view that obesity and weight is directly caused by dieting [5]. This reductive perspective overlooks the multilayered complexity of obesity involving genetic, biological, metabolic, medical, and psychological aspects, as well as the distinctive characteristics of Eds, which are characterized by the individual's dysfunctional relationship with food.

Nevertheless, comorbid EDs and obesity is a growing problem, as evident in population-based studies examining the co-occurrence of the two conditions irrespective of the prevalence increase in each of these conditions separately [15]. Individuals with co-occurring obesity and EDs are at higher risk for medical and psychosocial difficulties, such as more severe levels of depression and feelings of inadequacy [16].

While there are important distinctive characteristics between the two conditions, there is some research suggesting common etiological pathways and interactions between risk factors for obesity and EDs. The etiological factors of obesity and EDs are complex, multifactorial, and not yet fully understood. The EDIT trial (Eating Disorders In weight-related Therapy) aims to identify these shared risk factors and detect whether aspects of weight management interventions are individual predictors of ED risk [17]. For example, parental obesity, childhood obesity, and cultural and family factors that increase the likelihood of dieting and obesity are also risk factors for the development of BN and BED [18]. Similarly, eating behaviors such as loss of control eating, which is a characteristic of binge eating, is also linked with excess weight gain in community samples [19]. Dieting, use of media, body dissatisfaction, and experiences of weight-related teasing or bullying are also found to be shared risk factors for the development of eating and weight-related disorders [20].

Despite some shared risk factors, the mechanisms through which the two conditions link are not clear. Marcus [18] offers an overview of the possible linking mechanisms including psychiatric disorder (e.g., depression, attention deficit hyperactivity disorder), heritability [21], shared specific genes between obesity and EDs [22], hormonal factors such as abnormalities in the regulation of feeding behaviors, appetite and mood, or neurocognitive factors such as overactivity of reward systems in relation to food, which is also often used to fuel the hypothesis of food addiction [23, 24].

The aim of this chapter is to focus on two areas of comorbidity between the two conditions: body image and eating behaviors and how these manifest when the two conditions co-occur. It also aims to examine how treatment approaches should be adjusted in the face of contrasting treatment aims.

2. Body image

Excess body weight is often associated with impairments in quality of life, including an important aspect of psychosocial functioning: body image. Body dissatisfaction is also an important element in most EDs. In BN and AN, body dissatisfaction forms part of the diagnostic criteria, and even though it is not part of the diagnostic criteria for BED, there is emerging research that shows shape and weight concerns in individuals with BED comparable to those in individuals with BN and AN and higher body dissatisfaction than overweight controls without BED [25]. Body image, defined as the psychological experience of embodiment, represents any perceptions, thoughts, and feelings associated with one's experience of their own bodies [26]. Apart from the cognitive, emotional, and behavioral aspects, body image is also developed from historical influences (such as an individual's personality characteristics, parenting experiences, appearance-based teasing or bullying, and significance of body ideals in familial) and cultural-socialization experiences [27]. Although body image dissatisfaction is universal, it varies across different groups of individuals. For example, women are more likely to experience body image dissatisfaction [28, 29]; however, the manifestations of body image dissatisfaction can differ between genders (e.g., women seeking thinness, men seeking bulkiness) [30]. There are also differences between ethnic groups, where African American women report less body image dissatisfaction in comparison with European American women [31].

2.1 Body image and weight

Weight is not conclusively related to body image, and the mechanisms of action are not clear [32]. Even though there are some studies suggesting body image dissatisfaction being positively associated with excess body weight, this is not consistent [33, 34]. This aligns with the idea that body image is often irrespective of one's objective appearance. This is also evident through the finding that almost 50% of women report dissatisfaction with certain parts of their body (i.e., waist and abdomen) regardless of weight, aligning with cultural body ideals of thinness and femininity [35].

In a widely cited review article on obesity and body image, Schwartz and Brownell identified that obesity is linked with poor body image, but not everyone with obesity will struggle with poor body image or is equally susceptible to body dissatisfaction [36]. Some of the risk factors that increase the likelihood of body dissatisfaction they identified included being female, early onset obesity, or the presence of binge eating. There is accumulating evidence that individuals with BED also tend to experience body dissatisfaction that is further associated with greater eating-specific and general psychopathology [37]. Rizzo et al. have identified that higher BMI is associated with higher body dissatisfaction; however, higher BMI was not indicative of the presence of EDs in their sample [5]. Body dissatisfaction is the highest risk factor for the presence of EDs in adolescents, followed by depression and low self-esteem [38].

Interestingly, studies have found that adding a body image treatment component in traditional weight loss interventions does not improve body image outcomes; however, when body image interventions are offered as standalone treatment to overweight populations, there is significant body image and binge eating improvements in the absence of significant weight loss [39, 40]. A large study in Italy showed that body dissatisfaction, weight control, and eating behaviors are central in the presentation of ED symptoms and the internalization of weight stigma [41].

2.2 Body image and weight stigma

Weight stigma is any negative attitude, belief, or stereotype that associates higher weight with negative characteristics and manifests in discrimination against a person based on their weight or shape [42]. When an individual upholds these associations toward their own body weight, they experience internalized weight stigma. The presence and intensity of internalized weight stigma is strongly associated with greater ED symptoms, body dissatisfaction, and lower quality of life [43]. The experience of weight stigma can lead to increased risk for depression, anxiety, low self-esteem, poor body image, substance abuse, and suicidality, regardless of BMI, which indicates that these consequences are linked to the stigmatizing experiences themselves rather than weight [44–46]. It is not unusual that individuals experiencing internalized weight stigma get stuck in unhelpful vicious cycles of unhealthy behaviors such as binge eating or harmful ways of trying to control weight (e.g., through excessive nutritional restriction, excessive exercise, or laxative abuse), which prevents them from engaging in healthy weight loss practices and further adds to the stigmatizing experiences and low mood.

There are some studies that indicate that weight loss is associated with improvements in mood and can often protect against the presence of depression [47]. Faulconbridge outlines a number of mechanisms that possibly contribute to improvements in mood following weight loss in individuals with obesity [48]. These include a personal sense of accomplishment and pride at the weight loss progress, improvements in self-esteem, improvements in quality of life [49], and reduction in prejudice and social stigma. It is challenging to decipher the true effects of weight loss on mood given the multitude of factors that are involved in mood improvement in individuals with obesity. However, it is a crucial undertaking given that individuals and healthcare professionals often focus solely on weight loss by any means without investigating the underlying reasons for improvement that can fuel further weight stigma. Consequently, the role of weight loss can be exaggerated, to the point that individuals believe that their lives will improve in every possible aspect solely through weight loss, causing unrealistic expectations and creating fertile ground for disappointment, self-deprecation, and loss of motivation and meaning in weight management, as well as internalized weight stigma.

The reduction in prejudice and social stigma is certainly a positive effect of weight loss, but it can also highlight to individuals that they are treated differently when they experience weight loss, which can also lead to mood deteriorations as a result of weight stigma. Therefore, it raises the question of whether the intervention on prejudice and social stigma should be in the individual or societal attitudes toward obesity [50]. Marshall, Latner, and Masuda examined the link between internalized weight bias and disordered eating by analyzing the mediating role of drive for thinness and body image avoidance. Internalized weight bias was positively associated with disordered eating, and that drive for thinness and body image avoidance play a significant mediating role in this relationship [51].

Weight stigma, especially when internalized, can affect the individual's ability to seek support and treatment, increasing feelings of guilt, shame, and self-blame. There is a plethora of studies identifying the significant social stigma that is associated with obesity. Unfortunately, this has also been identified among healthcare professionals who may overdiagnose EDs in individuals with obesity, leading to occasionally overlooking other important medical or metabolic factors that may be contributing to an individual's difficulties with weight. On the other hand, there is also research indicating that individuals struggling with obesity may also experience delays in receiving ED diagnoses or treatment, which worsens their prognosis [52] either because of patients delaying or avoiding treatment due to past negative experiences with healthcare professionals [53] or because of misdiagnoses by healthcare professionals who often reinforce ED cognitions by focusing on and praising weight loss [54]. There is also evidence indicating that individuals with EDs can also be misdiagnosed based on healthcare professionals' weight bias, particularly in cases of atypical AN [55]. Atypical AN is often perceived as less severe due to the higher weight that individuals present with, which can often lead to a delay in accessing treatment [56]. Studies have found that overvaluation of weight and shape by the patient and weight history are better indicators of AN symptomatology than weight and BMI [57, 58]. Inappropriate diagnosing leads to inappropriate treatments that often place weight loss at the center of the intervention, rather than the patient's overall health [46, 59].

Studies have also identified significant weight bias among healthcare professionals, both physicians and mental health professionals, leading to reluctance to provide routine medical care, spend less time with overweight patients, or be more critical of them [60, 61]. Weight bias is also evident among healthcare professionals in ED services, where practitioners report more negative comments about higher-weight patients, feel more uncomfortable treating patients with obesity, or hold negative stereotypes about higher-weight patients [62]. McEntee et al. propose that weight stigma is one of the primary drivers for the suboptimal effectiveness of current ED treatments [63]. Weight stigma and discriminatory behaviors exacerbate or even cause these mental health difficulties [64] and are risk factors for the development of EDs [65]. Internalized weight stigma can even moderate ED treatment outcomes [66].

Interestingly, in a 2018 systematic review, it was found that weight stigma predicted elevation of biomarkers associated with hypothalamic-pituitary-adrenal axis reactivity, systemic inflammation, and type 2 diabetes [46]. Similarly, other studies found that the experience of weight stigma was correlated with a 60% increase in risk of mortality, beyond the mortality risk explained by BMI and other behavioral or health risk factors [67]. These findings highlight the difficulty in deciphering the true mechanisms of improvements in physical and psychological well-being observed with weight loss that is often used as an argument for weight-centric treatment approaches.

Therefore, it is evident that the relationship among obesity, weight loss, body image and dissatisfaction, EDs, and mood is complex. There is an important variable of the experience of internalized and external weight stigma that has only been recognized in the recent literature as a putative mechanism for the positive effects of weight loss on improvements in quality of life and mood. This is an important finding in order to challenge the all-encompassing and occasionally blind drive toward weight loss at all costs that is a precursor to EDs and disordered eating behaviors.

3. Eating habits and dieting

One of the most common areas of concern in comorbid obesity and EDs is the approach toward weight loss and eating habits. On one hand, healthcare professionals treating EDs are concerned about an overvaluation of weight loss and eating regimes that are largely driven by an idealization of thinness; on the other hand, healthcare professionals in the realm of obesity argue for the benefits of weight loss and maintaining a healthy weight [68].

3.1 Dieting and eating disorders

Dieting for weight loss is highly prevalent in cultures that value thinness, and the diet business is flourishing. However, the assumption that dieting yields long-term weight loss and increased physical health has been challenged by increasing evidence that shows its limited effectiveness in long-term results, as well as its potential risk of unintentional weight gain, disorders eating behaviors, and Eds—in fact dieting been found to be a shared risk factor between obesity and EDs [69]. Dieting can precede the onset of EDs and disordered eating, including binge eating, clinical and subthreshold EDs. Not every dieter will develop an ED, but it is rare that people with EDs do not report dieting at some point in their lives [70]. EDs are multifactorial and complex, and it is unlikely that dieting alone causes an ED. However, dieting itself might reinforce rigidity and cognitive control of food intake and may reinforce unhelpful attitudes and beliefs within social contexts that overvalue thinness through the reaction of the social environment on impact of dieting (e.g., compliments on weight loss).

3.2 Dieting and weight regain

Dieting has also been shown to be associated with long-term weight gain, which can also be a risk factor for EDs in the context of a weight stigmatizing environment. For example, a large longitudinal study found that in adolescents who dieted, their BMI was twice as much compared to adolescents who did not diet during that time [71]. There are several possible explanations for this relationship between dieting and long-term weight gain. Firstly, dieting is often associated with rigid control of eating and nutritional restriction at the expense of long-term sustainable changes to eating habits. These rigid rules are against what human bodies require to function optimally, and most individuals struggle to maintain these rules in the long-term, leading to weight gain. In addition, another variable that exacerbates this process is metabolic efficiency. When one's body receives suboptimal nutrition, the metabolic rate slows down in the body's attempt to survive a starvation period. As a result, one needs fewer calories (i.e., energy) to maintain their current weight. In combination with short-term, unsustainable rigid nutritional rules, periods between dieting lead to weight gain that is very common in individuals who experience repeat dieting. Furthermore, rigid nutritional control leads to extreme hunger, which is a risk factor for overeating and binge eating. When one breaks the rigid rules of dieting, it may be accompanied by feelings of failure or guilt that are often linked with comfort eating. Therefore, in some cases, dieting may also perpetuate a vicious cycle of negative emotions around food and body image that exacerbates the negative effects of dieting. Lastly, there are some important studies that indicate the impact of cognitive control of nutritional intake in comparison with physiological or intuitive control of nutritional intake (e.g., hunger), where cognitive control is more likely to lead to disinhibition around foods that were deemed forbidden [72, 73]. Another famous study from the 1950s also showed the detrimental effects of starvation on one's mood, cognitions around food, social relations, bingeing behaviors, and long-term weight gain [74]. These key studies often inform the treatment of EDs and obesity. In practice, it is very likely that all the above mechanisms operate simultaneously to prevent long-term weight loss when one diets.

There is some evidence indicating that there is not a consistent relationship between *medically supervised* dietary restriction and BED [75]. There are also studies indicating that severe dietary restriction under medical supervision (e.g., very low-calorie diets such as total dietary replacements) was not linked with binge eating and even reduced binge-eating behaviors [76, 77]. Therefore, it is possible that dietary restriction alone does not exacerbate EDs, without the presence of other risk factors such as experience of weight stigma, mood difficulties, family history of EDs, personality characteristics, family interactions and interpersonal dynamics, and food insecurity, among others [78–80]. It also highlights the importance of professional support in individuals who wish to lose weight through nutritional restriction and suffer with BED.

3.3 Dieting and physical health conditions

There is a large body of evidence suggesting the importance of weight loss on the prevention and improvement of health conditions associated with obesity such as Type 2 diabetes mellitus [81]. Type 2 diabetes is an impairment of the body's regulatory mechanism (i.e., the hormone insulin) for the amount of sugar (or glucose) in the bloodstream. The pancreas is not producing enough insulin, and at the same time, blood cells respond poorly to insulin, leading to increased levels of glucose in the bloodstream, which is associated with circulatory, nervous, and immune system conditions [82]. Type 2 diabetes, when monitored, can be prevented as blood glucose levels increase; therefore, there is an important window where prevention is possible. Often, during this period, lifestyle interventions are recommended as a first-line intervention to address the presence of risk factors for diabetes such as obesity or reduced physical activity. Research such as the Diabetes Prevention Program [83, 84] found overwhelming evidence that the incidence of diabetes was reduced by lifestyle intervention (i.e., healthy low-calorie and low-fat eating plan as well as at least 150 minutes of physical activity per week) in those with high risk of developing diabetes, more so than pharmacological management of diabetes. Interestingly, follow-up analyses indicated that it was weight loss that was primarily driving the reduction in diabetes risk, rather than lifestyle changes. These findings have been replicated in a number of other large-scale empirical studies such as the Finnish Diabetes Prevention study and the Da Qing study [85, 86]. Weight loss has also been shown to be beneficial for the reversal of Type 2 diabetes, although the evidence there is less conclusive. Large trials such as the look AHEAD trial have found that participants in the lifestyle intervention arm, compared to the structured education program, were more likely to achieve complete or partial remission from diabetes [87]. Interestingly, however, lifestyle intervention and weight loss did not make a significant difference in cardiovascular outcomes and mortality. It is not conclusively clear how weight loss is linked with overall mortality. This may be explained by the difficulty distinguishing intentional and unintentional weight loss. At the same time, rapid weight loss has also been associated with other health problems such as gallstones and cholecystitis, muscle strength, and bone density.

On the other hand, it is important to note that while BMI and weight are correlated with some physical health conditions like Type 2 diabetes and cardiovascular conditions, there are other factors such as weight cycling or other health behaviors that could also explain these observed associations between weight and these health conditions [88, 89]. Despite a large body of evidence indicating the effectiveness of weight loss interventions in improving cardiometabolic health, there could be other underlying mechanisms of action, such as the *behaviors* themselves that lead to weight loss (e.g., increasing physical movement, improvements in nutritional intake among others) [63]. There is evidence showing the superiority of health-improving behaviors over weight loss in improving overall health [90, 91]. There are also studies that examine weight loss without behavioral changes (e.g., with liposuction or bariatric surgery) that show limited effectiveness of pure weight loss on physical health improvements [92, 93].

In summary, weight management seems to have a significant effect on the prevention and partially on the remission of type 2 diabetes and other physical health conditions associated with obesity. However, studies that support this hypothesis do not consistently define the means through which weight loss is achieved. It is important to identify the mechanisms through which weight loss impacts the effectiveness of prevention and treatment of obesity-related health conditions to avoid unnecessarily weight-centric approaches, since it is becoming increasingly evident that behavioral and lifestyle changes play an important role in this process.

Table 1 summarizes the main areas of comorbidity and association between EDs and obesity.

Comorbidity aspects	Main conclusions	Controversy	Key reference
Body image	• Main risk factors for body dissatisfaction include being female, early onset, and binge eating *but not body weight (or obesity)* • Body dissatisfaction is a key risk factor for the development of EDs • Increasing evidence of body image disturbance in individuals with BED	Individuals with obesity will not necessarily struggle with body dissatisfaction but when they do, they are at increased risk for EDs. The mechanisms through which excess weight links with body image are not clear and may be more associated with stigmatizing experiences, social pressures, and eating behaviors rather than weight itself.	[36]
Weight stigma	• Experiences of weight stigma and internalized weight stigma are associated with increased risk for mental disorders and EDs, and even moderate ED treatment, outcomes *regardless of BMI* • Weight stigma is found to be associated with physical health metrics and mortality risk • Improvements in mood associated with weight loss may be better explained by reduction in stigmatizing experiences and increased social connectedness • Weight bias in healthcare professionals can lead to misdiagnosis and delays in treatment	The extensive role of weight stigmatizing experiences is largely overlooked in obesity and ED treatments, when internalized weight stigma is a key driver in the development of EDs. Patients with obesity and comorbid EDs are often misdiagnosed and overlooked as symptomatology is often assumed to be caused solely by weight.	[45, 46]
Dieting and eating behaviors	• Dieting is linked with long-term weight gain and increased risk for EDs • Inconsistent evidence about medically supervised dieting and binge-eating behaviors • Weight loss is associated with improvements in physical health conditions such as type 2 diabetes, although these improvements may also be due to the behavioral changes associated with weight loss (e.g., physical activity increases)	Weight loss through dieting is not appropriate for individuals with obesity and EDs given its impact on cognitive control and rigidity, which may perpetuate ED cognitions. Nutritional interventions should be integrated into a holistic care plan that does not promote controversial messages about importance of weight. There is inconsistent evidence about the appropriateness of medically supervised dieting and EDs.	[69]

Table 1.
Summary of associations between obesity and EDs.

4. Implications on treatment and recommendations for balanced interventions

Clinicians treating patients with obesity are increasingly treating comorbid EDs and vice versa. However, despite the increased and evidenced co-occurrence of the two conditions and the evidenced medical and psychosocial risks of their comorbidity, there is significant debate among healthcare professionals with regards to the most appropriate course of treatment. It is imperative that clinicians in both areas are familiar with obesity-related medical morbidity and its psychosocial correlates, how EDs might present and are treated, and are able to refer appropriately.

4.1 Weight management and eating disorders

While obesity interventions are necessary for the promotion of health, as indicated by the research presented in this chapter, it should not be founded in the false attribution of blame to the affected individuals. Weight is influenced by a number of different variables (e.g., genetics, neurobiology, social environment), and eating behaviors is only one of these. Weight is not consistently linked with eating behaviors, but more so with body image and body dissatisfaction, which can prove fertile ground for mental health difficulties and EDs [5]. Weight is not a behavior, and weight does not equate health. Best practice recommendations include behavior modification that does not focus on weight but specific behaviors that promote health and well-being without focusing on weight loss [94]. There needs to be a shift in treatment to healthy eating and physical activity increase for long-term sustainability. Despite this, dieting remains high, possibly due to lack of alternative options for sustainable weight loss offered by public health [69].

Weight-centric approaches have been criticized for pathologizing excess body fat influenced partly by the idealization of thinness societal ideals, blaming the individual while ignoring the substantial impact of the obesogenic environment that individuals operate in [95–98]. More recently, weight-neutral approaches have started gaining ground in their effectiveness in managing both physical health complications and psychosocial components of EDs and obesity, although there remains a lack of guidance on how these can be applied to EDs [99–102]. Guidelines published in Australia for the management of EDs in people with higher weight outline that psychological therapy should be offered to all individuals with EDs first, with the addition of a specific focus on weight stigma and its implications on the individual's life, on multidisciplinary approaches, and on the important consideration of cultural influences [103].

Although these guidelines remain cautious about the application of weight loss interventions in individuals with EDs, they highlight the relationship between short-term weight loss and ED relapse. While they acknowledge that non-supervised weight loss programs are not recommended for people with EDs, they explain that there is no consensus on whether an individual with an ED should attempt a medically supervised weight loss program. They recommend that weight-neutral approaches are considered given the similar health benefits they present to weight-centric approaches.

Research indicates that in individuals with BED, weight loss outcomes following weight management interventions are modest and show reduced long-term maintenance compared to controls with obesity without BED [104, 105]. It has also been suggested that ED treatments for BED do not result in weight loss, whereas weight management interventions do [106]. However, considering emerging evidence about the effectiveness of weight-neutral interventions, it is important to examine other aspects at play in the development and maintenance of BED and obesity and how the interplay may affect the long-term maintenance of results both in relation to weight loss and binge-eating behaviors. Therefore, although weight loss programs are not contraindicated for people experiencing BED, it may be more beneficial to address binge-eating behaviors prior to pursuing weight loss, in order to avoid the exacerbation of loss-of-control eating through the imposed and/or perceived restriction often experienced in weight loss programs and to increase the probability of long-term maintenance.

It is also important to note that when healthcare professionals ignore the perceived or actual need for weight management, patients can often disagree with the treatment focus and at worst disengage from treatment [107]. This highlights the importance of a thorough and individualized assessment and formulation of the patient and the incorporation of a weight-neutral approach at a pace that feels comfortable and appropriate for each patient. Similarly, healthcare professionals specializing in obesity should not ignore the presence of disordered eating behaviors to ensure long-term sustainable results and offer more personalized care while understanding the patients' deeper relationship with their eating behaviors [107].

With regards to weight monitoring, although it is a crucial element in ED treatment models, it can often fuel the unhelpful belief that weight is the main indicator of health. According to McEntee et al., there have not been any dismantling studies to investigate the utility of regular weigh-ins in ED interventions [63]. Of course, weight restoration is a crucial treatment component in AN. However, there is limited evidence toward what target weight should be [108]. Therefore, concrete and easily observable measures such as BMI are used to define "recovery" that ranges from unhealthy to healthy to overweight, which is often confusing for patients who are working to change their relationship with food and their bodies. McEntee et al. propose that if weigh-ins are required in ED treatment, that their purpose needs to be communicated clearly and how they form part of a comprehensive treatment plan, which also includes addressing internalized weight stigma [63].

4.2 Bariatric surgery and eating disorders

Bariatric surgery usually yields the best outcomes in relation to weight loss and is considered the most effective intervention for severe obesity as measured by BMI. However, bariatric surgery outcomes can be complicated when there is comorbid ED symptomatology [109]. It is reported that up to 50% of bariatric surgery candidates report some form of disordered eating, most commonly loss of control in eating [110], and 5–15% of candidates may struggle with BED [111].

There is accumulating research on the effectiveness of bariatric surgery in reducing binge-eating symptoms, as well as on the impact of binge eating pre-surgery on the effectiveness of long-term weight outcomes post-surgery. Some studies indicate that patients with BED have equally effective outcomes post-surgery [112], while others highlight the increased post-operative complications, reduced weight loss, and increased weight regain in patients with BED undergoing bariatric surgery [113–117]. However, because the weight loss post-surgery with BED is far superior to non-surgical treatments for obesity, the presence of BED is still not considered a contraindication for bariatric surgery [118]. In practice, there is a general consensus that ED symptoms should be treated first before patients undergo bariatric surgery due to the poor weight loss prognosis when these symptoms are present pre-surgery [119].

Loss-of-control eating and binge-eating behaviors have been found to affect weight loss outcome post-surgery negatively. It was identified that protective factors for loss of control eating and binge eating in a post-bariatric surgery population included increased self-monitoring of eating, higher daily eating frequency, older age and male gender, as well as higher self-esteem [113]. Despite the evidenced impact of weight stigma and body dissatisfaction in disordered eating, there is limited research investigating the impact of these factors on surgery outcomes [118]. While there is some research on the positive impact of surgery on body image and psychosocial issues [120], there is still an important fraction of patients who struggle with body dissatisfaction and romantic and sexual relationships post-surgery, particularly at the timepoint when their weight stops shifting [118]. This indicates the importance of psychological work pre- and post-surgery to ensure the best long-term outcomes, as well as the importance of psychological assessments prior to surgery and personalized care plans in patients with BED undergoing surgery [118, 121]. Some studies have found that adding a psychological component such as acceptance and commitment therapy (ACT) can support reversal of weight regain post-surgery, although their population did not distinguish between patients with and without disordered eating or BED [122, 123].

There have been some suggestions that bariatric surgery links with the development of EDs or disordered eating post-surgery in some rare occasions, particularly atypical AN [124]. However, the data are very limited and primarily based on case studies [125, 126]. It has also been challenging to operationalize ED symptomatology in patients who have undergone bariatric surgery, given that some symptoms that would otherwise be classified under ED diagnoses are expected and common in bariatric surgery patients (e.g., rapid weight loss, concerns regarding weight and eating) [127]. This is an important area of future research, given that it has been suggested that there may be critical weight loss thresholds that can identify bariatric patients at risk of EDs post-surgery [124], but there has been extremely limited research on the psychological components of the development of EDs post-surgery.

4.3 Psychological treatments

There is a substantial body of evidence showing the effectiveness of adding cognitive-behavioral therapy (CBT) in weight loss treatments in reducing binge-eating behaviors as well as BMI, in comparison to weight loss treatments alone [128–131]. However, CBT targets binge-eating behaviors and does not encourage weight loss in individuals with comorbid obesity. Similarly, weight loss therapies do not target specifically binge-eating behaviors. Therefore, it is no surprise that CBT alone does not lead to significant weight loss [132]. In patients with comorbid obesity and EDs, it is important to address the psychological components first before or concurrently with behavioral weight loss interventions to ensure better long-term outcomes.

McEntee et al. propose that "fear of fatness," an essential component of the transdiagnostic model of EDs, is not explicitly targeted in CBT, and when it is, it is primarily with the aim to challenge beliefs of fatness, further fueling the demonization of excess weight [63]. Inadvertently, body image is addressed in ways that can fuel fat-phobic attitudes and perpetuate the negative consequences of experienced and internalized weight stigma. Therefore, it is crucial to reframe some of the stigmatizing language used in CBT (e.g., "you are not fat, you feel fat"), which operates under the assumption that fatness is bad.

Furthermore, adding a component where weight stigma and the effectiveness of weight-centric approach is challenged may also be helpful. Approaches such as ACT or compassion-focused therapy (CFT) may prove useful allies in shifting the paradigm toward a more health-focused, weight-neutral practice that places health and wellbeing at the center of the intervention regardless of one's weight [63]. More specifically, ACT can facilitate a more accepting perspective of the complexity of body and weight while also encouraging commitment and lifestyle changes that can improve physical and psychological health more holistically both in EDs and obesity. Similarly, CFT can encourage the development of a more understanding and caring perspective toward one's experience of weight stigma and body image. This creates the space for a more person-focused choice of where the individual wishes to intervene, beyond the influence of weight-stigmatizing experiences. Self-criticism and self-blame are usual suspects in the maintenance of eating-related difficulties and body image difficulties [133]; therefore, a CFT approach lends itself well to challenging some of these components before a collaborative care plan is established.

4.4 Pharmacotherapy for weight loss

In the last few years, there have been important developments in the arena of weight loss medications (e.g., GLP-1 antagonists) that enter more powerfully than ever into the toolbox of weight management healthcare professionals to support people who struggle losing weight solely with traditional behavioral methods. However, these new medications have not been approved yet for use with individuals with EDs [134, 135], despite some preliminary evidence that they may reduce binge-eating behaviors [136].

This group of medications must remain a tool for healthcare professionals to aid people who struggle with clinical obesity and have not been able to lose weight for health reasons with behavioral and lifestyle change approaches. As evidenced above, weight loss regimes (including pharmacotherapy) will do very little if they are not combined with behavioral and lifestyles changes, alongside the right support from healthcare specialists. Weight loss medications do not alleviate the impact that psychological, societal, and systemic factors have on the development of obesity in the first place and certainly do not mitigate any ED risk. It is concerning how weight loss medications have been introduced in the media as the "new wonder drugs" for weight loss and how celebrities who do not struggle with clinical obesity have used these "in preparation for awards season" to slim down. The promotion of pharmacotherapy in this way is very concerning, as it reinforces unhelpful ideas about the meaning of weight and associated stigma and can have detrimental effects on the maintenance of EDs [135].

It is difficult to strike the right balance between supporting people who struggle with clinical obesity and not reinforcing and perpetuating unfair and unhelpful weight stereotypes and stigma that can fuel EDs. It is important to continue the research on finding the right tools and helping people with clinical obesity. However, as discussed above, healthcare professionals have to be careful not to fall into weight stigma traps that exploit the rife fatphobia in our society. Bartel et al. summarize helpful guidance on how to approach use of GLP-1s in patients with active EDs, including an exploration of reasons behind the use of GLP-1 medications (including weight discrimination), a thorough education about how GLP-1 medications work, a discussion about how GLP-1 medications can impact ED treatment (e.g., by reinforcing avoidance of food, avoidance of weight and body image), and the inclusion of the use of GLP-1 medication to the case conceptualization [135].

4.5 Addressing weight stigma in healthcare professionals

The importance of internalized and experienced weight stigma in obesity and EDs has been shown. However, in practice, ED treatments offer little focus on the exploration of weight stigma experiences and the social constructs that often fuel the

ED symptomatology. Practice guidelines offer little support to clinicians in treating comorbid obesity and EDs [103].

It is important for healthcare professionals to create a judgment-free, empathetic, and attentive environment and relationship where the patient can feel comfortable and understood. Healthcare professionals should remain open and curious toward the patient's experiences to fully understand and formulate the different individual, biological, medical, and societal components that may contribute to the problem they present with. In order to achieve this, healthcare professionals should allow enough time to fully assess current and historical eating and dieting behaviors and educate the patient on the physiological and psychological impact of long-term dieting, their social environments and social relationships, and triggers for dieting or eating behaviors. The treatment aim should be flexibility around food and reducing the power of the weight on the individual's self-esteem and body perception. The focus should be on health-promoting behaviors and increasing the individual's self-efficacy and access to healthcare systems. The purpose of weight loss and weight management should be examined with each individual separately, and weighing should have a clear rationale in ED and obesity treatment.

Clinicians can reflect on their own attitudes in relation to excess weight and understand the importance of weight stigma in the experience of people living with obesity. Healthcare professionals should be trained on weight-neutral approaches and work collaboratively with individuals to create shared care plans. In order to support themselves and the patients to move away from weight-centric approaches, functional measures of progress should be used instead of weight or BMI (e.g., improvements in mood, sleep, energy levels, mobility etc.). On a societal level, policies should be reviewed with newer research and data, acknowledging and addressing the societal determinants of obesity rather than solely focusing on the provision of weight management approaches. Healthcare professionals should also be encouraged to identify

Treatment aspects	Main conclusions	Controversy	Key reference
Weight management	• Weight-centric approaches have been criticized for pathologizing excess weight whilst ignoring the impact of the obesogenic environment • Weight-neutral approaches are gaining ground; however, there is limited guidance for application within EDs • Weight monitoring and achieving a "healthy weight" as a crucial component in ED treatment is challenged as it can be confusing for patients and can exacerbate thinness ideals	There is inconclusive evidence about the effectiveness of weight management interventions in individuals with BED or other EDs. It is generally suggested that EDs are treated first prior to a weight management intervention, but guidance about appropriateness of weight management interventions in EDs is limited.	[137]

Treatment aspects	Main conclusions	Controversy	Key reference
Bariatric surgery	• The effectiveness of bariatric surgery outcomes can be affected by the presence of disordered eating or BED • Psychological work before and after surgery may be crucial to support patients with body dissatisfaction, internalized weight stigma, and disordered eating behaviors • Despite limited evidence, there is a rare occurrence of the development of EDs post-bariatric surgery	Despite BED not being a contraindication for bariatric surgery, given the poor prognosis for positive weight loss results, it is often recommended that it is treated first before patients are offered bariatric surgery. There is limited understanding of the development of EDs post-surgery given that ED diagnostic criteria do not fit bariatric surgery patients.	[118]
Psychological treatments	• CBT and other psychological treatments have been shown to be effective in reducing BED symptomatology in patients with comorbid obesity • CBT approaches to body image can often fuel weight bias inadvertently	It is unclear which intervention should be prioritized in individuals with comorbid obesity and EDs; however, it is often shown that addressing psychological components first can yield longer-term results in weight management.	[121]
Pharmaco-therapy	• New developments in pharmacotherapy for weight loss give new tools for professionals to treat obesity; however, these need to be used carefully with patients with EDs as the evidence remains limited • Effects of pharmacotherapy could limit effectiveness of ED treatments	There is limited guidance for the use of pharmacotherapy in the treatment of comorbid EDs and obesity. It is important to consider the impact of how weight loss medications are promoted on the maintenance and possible development of EDs.	[134]
Weight bias in healthcare professionals	• Healthcare professionals are usually offered little support in reflecting on their own weight biases • It is important to understand weight-neutral approaches	Weight bias in healthcare professionals can have an impact on the choice of treatment and therapeutic alliance with the patient. Particularly if ED symptomatology is present, patients can often be discouraged to seek support, or weight-biased internalized beliefs may be exacerbated.	[63]

Table 2.
Summary of treatment areas of association between obesity and EDs.

and possibly address research and clinical gaps to investigate the effectiveness of weight-neutral approaches on the long-term health outcomes of individuals with obesity and or EDs [63].

	Recommendations for practice
Weight management	• Focus treatment on behavior modification and health-promoting behaviors in line with patient values rather than weight loss. • Avoid prescribing dieting and rigid regimes. • Consider whether treatment of BED and other EDs needs to be prioritized first. • Individualize assessments and formulations to ensure a weight-neutral approach is implemented at a pace appropriate for the patient and their beliefs. • If weight monitoring is needed as part of weight restoration in EDs or obesity, it should be explicitly discussed with the patient how it forms part of a larger holistic care plan.
Bariatric surgery	• Where possible, offer pre- and post-surgery psychological assessment and support. • Individualize care plans in bariatric surgery candidates and assess suitability with the consideration of psychological factors, too. • Assess risk for development of EDs post-bariatric surgery.
Psychological treatments	• Encourage engagement in psychological work prior or concurrently with weight management interventions. • Use alternative models such as ACT and CFT to encourage a more individualized approach to areas of psychological intervention. • Avoid assumptions that individuals with obesity will experience body dissatisfaction. • Explore sensitively and collaboratively the influences of body dissatisfaction in each individual regardless of weight.
Pharmacotherapy	• Assess carefully the appropriateness of use of pharmacotherapy in patients with comorbid Eds. • Monitor ED symptomatology, including psychological components of body dissatisfaction and internalized weight stigma, throughout pharmacotherapy treatment. • Discuss with patient about mechanism of action of GLP-1 medications and monitor impact on ED symptomatology.
Weight bias in healthcare professionals	• Reflect on own values and beliefs around weight and body. • Encourage training of healthcare professionals on weight-neutral approaches and avoid placing weight at the center of the intervention. • Create a judgment-free and empathetic environment for the patient to feel comfortable and understood. • Explore experiences of weight stigma and impact on eating behaviors and relationship with body early on in treatment. • Use functional measures of progress instead of weight or BMI. • Review of policies to address social determinants of obesity. • Encourage societal and individual interventions on weight attitudes and stigma.

Table 3.
Summary of recommendations for practice in the treatment of comorbid EDs and obesity.

Table 2 summarizes the associated treatment areas between obesity and EDs.

Table 3 summarizes the recommendations for practice in the treatment of comorbid EDs and obesity.

5. Conclusion

It is evident that a greater exchange of knowledge and experience between healthcare professionals working in EDs and obesity is essential [107], although the highly specialized, tiered healthcare system often poses a barrier to this highly valuable exchange. In addition, there is need for greater integration between different healthcare professions, considering that in obesity, healthcare professionals are mostly from a medical or nutritional background, in comparison to healthcare professionals in EDs who tend to be more psychologically trained. Integrated treatments may also facilitate treatment access for individuals with EDs with comorbid obesity, as individuals are less likely to see treatment for EDs compared to obesity [6]. Ultimately, both fields share the goal of helping individuals with acknowledging problematic eating behaviors and developing a healthier relationship with food and their bodies.

Conflict of interest

The authors declare no conflict of interest.

Author details

Iakovina Koutoufa
National Health Service, UK

*Address all correspondence to: ikoutoufa@gmail.com

References

[1] American Psychiatric Association. Diagnostic and Statistical Manual of Mental Disorders. 5th ed. Arlington, VA: American Psychiatric Publishing; 2013

[2] American Psychiatric Association. Diagnostic and Statistical Manual of Mental Disorders. 3rd ed. Washington, DC: American Psychiatric Press; 1980

[3] Kessler RC, Haro JM, Heeringa SG, Pennell BE, Üstün TB. The World Health Organization world mental health survey initiative. Epidemiology and Psychiatric Sciences. 2006;**15**(3):161-166

[4] Setayesh T et al. Impact of obesity and overweight on DNA stability: Few facts and many hypotheses. Mutation Research. 2018;777:64-91

[5] Rizzo A et al. Obesity and eating disorders: Evidences for differentiation. KMAN Counseling & Psychology Nexus. 2025;**In press**:10-19

[6] Palavras MA, Kaio GH, Mari J, Claudino AM. A review of Latin American studies on binge eating disorder. Brazilian Journal of Psychiatry. 2011;**33**:s81-s94

[7] Udo T, Grilo CM. Prevalence and correlates of DSM-5–defined eating disorders in a nationally representative sample of U.S. adults. Biological Psychiatry. 2018;**84**(5):345-354

[8] World Health Organization. Obesity and Overweight [Online]. 2024. Available from: https://www.who.int/news-room/fact-sheets/detail/obesity-and-overweight [Accessed: December 27, 2024]

[9] Tanamas SK, Ng WL, Backholer K, Hodge A, Zimmet PZ, Peeters A. Quantifying the proportion of deaths due to body mass index-and waist circumference-defined obesity. Obesity. 2016;**24**(3):735-742

[10] Vranian M et al. The interaction of fitness, fatness, and cardiometabolic risk. Journal of the American College of Cardiology. 2012;**59**(13S):E1754-E1754

[11] Dehal A, Garrett T, Tedders SH, Arroyo C, Afriyie-Gyawu E, Zhang J. Body mass index and death rate of colorectal cancer among a national cohort of U.S. adults. Adult Nutrition. 2011;**63**(8):1218-1225

[12] Wang YC, McPherson K, Marsh T, Gortmaker SL, Brown M. Health and economic burden of the projected obesity trends in the USA and the UK. Lancet. 2011;**378**:815-825

[13] Perpina C, Roncero M. Similarities and differences between eating disorders and obese patients in a virtual environment for normalizing eating patterns. Comprehensive Psychiatry. 2016;**67**:39-45

[14] Mento C et al. Sex differences in emotions and eating behaviors among people affected by obesity. Brain Sciences. 2022;**12**(12):1663

[15] Da Luz FQ, Sainsbury A, Mannan H, Touyz S, Mitchison D, Hay P. Prevalence of obesity and comorbid eating disorder behaviors in South Australia from 1995 to 2015. International Journal of Obesity. 2017;**41**(7):1148-1153

[16] Poli R, Maninetti L, Bodini P, Agrimi E. Obesity, binge eating, obstruction sleep apnea and psychopathological features. Clinical Neuropsychiatry. 2012;**9**(4):166-170

[17] Lister NB et al. Eating disorders in weight-related therapy (EDIT) collaboration: Rationale and study design. Nutrition Research Reviews. 2024;**37**(1):32-42

[18] Marcus MD. Connections between eating disorders and obesity. In: Brownell KD, Walsh BT, editors. Eating Disorders and Obesity: A Comprehensive Handbook. 3rd ed. New York: Guilford Press; 2017. pp. 229-234

[19] Catania J, Spirou D, Gascoigne M, Raman J. Loss of control as a transdiagnostic feature in obesity-related eating behaviours: A systematic review. European Eating Disorders Review. 2023;**31**(1):24-45

[20] Haines J, Neumark-Sztainer D. Prevention of obesity and eating disorders: A consideration of shared risk factors. Health Education Research. 2006;**21**(6):770-782

[21] Campbell IC, Mill J, Uher R, Schmidt U. Eating disorders, gene–environment interactions and epigenetics. Neuroscience and Biobehavioral Reviews. 2011;**35**(3):784-793

[22] Müller TD et al. Fat mass and obesity-associated gene (FTO) in eating disorders: Evidence for association of the rs9939609 obesity risk allele with bulimia nervosa and anorexia nervosa. Obesity Facts. 2012;**5**(3):408-419

[23] Imperatori C, Mancini M, Della Marca G, Valenti EM, Farina B. Feedback-based treatments for eating disorders and related symptoms: A systematic review of the literature. Nutrients. 2018;**10**(11):1806

[24] Schmidt R et al. Neuropsychological and neurophysiological indicators of general and food-specific impulsivity in children with overweight and obesity: A pilot study. Nutrients. 2018;**10**(12):1983

[25] Grilo CM. Why no cognitive body image feature such as overvaluation of shape/weight in the binge eating disorder diagnosis? The International Journal of Eating Disorders. 2013;**46**(3):208-211

[26] Cash TF, Smolak L. Body Image: A Handbook of Science, Practice, and Prevention. 2nd ed. New York: Guildford Press; 2011

[27] Jarry JL, Cash TF. Cognitive-behavioural approaches to body image change. In: Cash TF, Smolak L, editors. Body Image: A Handbook of Science, Practice, and Prevention. 2nd ed. New York: Guilford Press; 2011. pp. 415-426

[28] Forbes GB, Adams-Curtis LE, Rade B, Jaberg P. Body dissatisfaction in women and men: The role of gender-typing and self-esteem. Sex Roles. 2001;**44**(7):461-484

[29] MacNeill LP, Best LA, Davis LL. The role of personality in body image dissatisfaction and disordered eating: Discrepancies between men and women. Journal of Eating Disorders. 2017;**5**(1):44

[30] McCabe MP, Ricciardelli LA. Body image dissatisfaction among males across the lifespan: A review of past literature. Journal of Psychosomatic Research. 2004;**56**(6):675-685

[31] Jefferson DL, Stake JE. Appearance self-attitudes of African American and European American women: Media comparisons and internalization of beauty ideals. Psychology of Women Quarterly. 2009;**33**(4):396-409

[32] Chao H-L. Body image change in obese and overweight persons enrolled in weight loss intervention programs:

A systematic review and meta-analysis. PLoS ONE. 2015;**10**(5):e0124036

[33] Sarwer DB, Thompson JK, Cash TF. Body image and obesity in adulthood. Psychiatria Clinica. 2005;**28**(1):69-87

[34] Sarwer DB, Wadden TA, Foster GD. Assessment of body image dissatisfaction in obese women: Specificity, severity, and clinical significance. Journal of Consulting and Clinical Psychology. 1998;**66**(4):651-654

[35] Bucchianeri MM, Arikian AJ, Hannan PJ, Eisenberg ME, Neumark-Sztainer D. Body dissatisfaction from adolescence to young adulthood: Findings from a 10-year longitudinal study. Body Image. 2013;**10**(1):1-7

[36] Schwartz MB, Brownell KD. Obesity and body image. Body Image. 2004;**1**(1):43-56

[37] Thompson JK, Schaefer L. Body image, obesity, and eating disorders. In: Brownell KD, Walsh BT, editors. Eating Disorders and Obesity: A Comprehensive Handbook. 3rd ed. New York: Guilford Press; 2017. pp. 140-144

[38] Suarez-Albor CL, Galletta M, Gómez-Bustamante EM. Factors associated with eating disorders in adolescents: A systematic review. Acta Bio-Medica. 2022;**93**(3):e2022253

[39] Ramirez EM, Rosen JC. A comparison of weight control and weight control plus body image therapy for obese men and women. Journal of Consulting and Clinical Psychology. 2001;**69**(3):440

[40] Carraça EV et al. Body image change and improved eating self-regulation in a weight management intervention in women. International Journal of Behavioral Nutrition and Physical Activity. 2011;**8**(1):75

[41] Calugi S et al. Weight bias internalization and eating disorder psychopathology in treatment-seeking patients with obesity. Nutrients. 2023;**15**(13):2932

[42] Hart LM, Ferreira KB, Ambwani S, Gibson EB, Austin SB. Developing expert consensus on how to address weight stigma in public health research and practice: A Delphi study 79. Stigma and Health. 2021;**6**(1):79-89

[43] Wagner AF, Butt M, Rigby A. Internalized weight bias in patients presenting for bariatric surgery. Eating Behaviors. 2020;**39**:101429

[44] Puhl RM. Stigma, discrimination, and obesity. In: Brownell KD, Walsh BT, editors. Eating Disorders and Obesity: A Comprehensive Handbook. 3rd ed. New York: Guilford Press; 2017. pp. 134-139

[45] Papadopoulos S, Brennan L. Correlates of weight stigma in adults with overweight and obesity: A systematic literature review. Obesity. 2015;**23**(9):1743-1760

[46] Wu Y-K, Berry DC. Impact of weight stigma on physiological and psychological health outcomes for overweight and obese adults: A systematic review. Journal of Advanced Nursing. 2018;**74**(5):1030-1042

[47] Faulconbridge LF et al. One-year changes in symptoms of depression and weight in overweight/obese individuals with type 2 diabetes in the look AHEAD study. Obesity. 2012;**20**(4):783-793

[48] Faulconbridge LF. Social and psychological effects of weight loss. In: Brownell KD, Walsh BT, editors. Eating Disorders and Obesity: A Comprehensive Handbook. 3rd ed. New York: Routledge; 2017. pp. 464-472

[49] Maciejewski ML, Patrick DL, Williamson DF. A structured review of randomized controlled trials of weight loss showed little improvement in health-related quality of life. Journal of Clinical Epidemiology. 2005;**58**(6):568-578

[50] Puhl RM, Himmelstein MS, Pearl RL. Weight stigma as a psychosocial contributor to obesity. The American Psychologist. 2020;**75**(2):274-289

[51] Marshall RD, Latner JD, Masuda A. Internalized weight bias and disordered eating: The mediating role of body image avoidance and drive for thinness. Frontiers in Psychology. 2020;**10**:2999

[52] Ratnasuriya RH, Eisler I, Szmukler GI, Russell GFM. Anorexia nervosa: Outcome and prognostic factors after 20 years. The British Journal of Psychiatry. 1991;**158**(4):495-502

[53] Mensinger JL, Tylka TL, Calamari ME. Mechanisms underlying weight status and healthcare avoidance in women: A study of weight stigma, body-related shame and guilt, and healthcare stress. Body Image. 2018;**25**:139-147

[54] Sim LA, McAlpine DE, Grothe KB, Himes SM, Cockerill RG, Clark MM. Identification and treatment of eating disorders in the primary care setting. Mayo Clinic Proceedings. 2010;**85**(8):746-751

[55] Harrop EN, Hutcheson R, Harner V, Mensinger JL, Lindhorst T. 'You don't look anorexic': Atypical anorexia patient experiences of weight stigma in medical care. Body Image. 2023;**46**:48-61

[56] Cunning A, Rancourt D. Stigmatization of anorexia nervosa versus atypical anorexia nervosa: An experimental study. Stigma and Health. 2024;**9**(3):249-257

[57] Dang AB et al. Assessing severity in anorexia nervosa: Do the DSM-5 and an alternative severity rating based on overvaluation of weight and shape severity differ in psychological and biological correlates? European Eating Disorders Review. 2023;**31**(4):447-461

[58] Garber AK et al. Weight loss and illness severity in adolescents with atypical anorexia nervosa. Pediatrics. 2019;**144**(6):e20192339

[59] Meyer L, Gram EG, Brodersen JB, Køster-Rasmussen R. Overdiagnosis in overweight. BMJ Evidence-Based Medicine. 2023;**28**(Suppl. 1):A26-A27

[60] Bertakis KD, Azari R. The impact of obesity on primary care visits. Obesity Research. 2005;**13**(9):1615-1623

[61] Hebl MR, Xu J, Mason MF. Weighing the care: Patients' perceptions of physician care as a function of gender and weight. International Journal of Obesity. 2003;**27**(2):269-275

[62] Puhl RM, Latner JD, King KM, Luedicke J. Weight bias among professionals treating eating disorders: Attitudes about treatment and perceived patient outcomes. The International Journal of Eating Disorders. 2014;**47**(1):65-75

[63] McEntee ML, Philip SR, Phelan SM. Dismantling weight stigma in eating disorder treatment: Next steps for the field. Frontiers in Psychiatry. 2023;**14**:1157594

[64] Puhl R, Brownell KD. Bias, discrimination and obesity. In: Grodin M, Tarantola D, Annas G, Gruskin S, editors. Health and Human Rights in a Changing World. 3rd ed. New York: Routledge; 2013. pp. 581-606

[65] Fairburn CG. Cognitive Behavior Therapy and Eating Disorders. New York, NY: The Guildford Press; 2008

[66] Mensinger JL, Calogero RM, Tylka TL. Internalized weight stigma moderates eating behavior outcomes in women with high BMI participating in a healthy living program. Appetite. 2016;**102**:32-43

[67] Sutin AR, Stephan Y, Terracciano A. Weight discrimination and risk of mortality. Psychological Science. 2015;**26**(11):1803-1811

[68] Sainsbury A, Hay P. Call for an urgent rethink of the 'health at every size' concept. Journal of Eating Disorders. 2014;**2**(1):8

[69] Neumark-Sztainer DR, Loth KA. The impact of dieting. In: Brownell KD, Walsh BT, editors. Eating Disorders and Obesity: A Comprehensive Handbook. 3rd ed. New York: Routledge; 2017. pp. 109-115

[70] Stice E, Presnell K. Dieting and the eating disorders. In: Agras WS, editor. The Oxford Handbook of Eating Disorders. New York: Oxford University Press; 2010. pp. 148-179

[71] Neumark-Sztainer D, Wall M, Story M, Standish AR. Dieting and unhealthy weight control behaviors during adolescence: Associations with 10-year changes in body mass index. Journal of Adolescent Health. 2012;**50**(1):80-86

[72] Polivy J, Herman CP. Dieting and binging: A causal analysis. The American Psychologist. 1985;**40**(2):193-201

[73] Polivy J. Psychological consequences of food restriction. Journal of the American Dietetic Association. 1996;**96**(6):589-592

[74] Keys A, Brozek J, Henschel A. The Biology of Human Starvation Volume 2. Minneapolis, MN, USA: University of Minnessota Press; 1950

[75] Howard CE, Porzelius LK. The role of dieting in binge eating disorder: Etiology and treatment implications. Clinical Psychology Review. 1999;**19**(1):25-44

[76] da Luz FQ et al. Does severe dietary energy restriction increase binge eating in overweight or obese individuals? A systematic review. Obesity Reviews. 2015;**16**(8):652-665

[77] Jebeile H et al. Eating disorder risk during behavioral weight management in adults with overweight or obesity: A systematic review with meta-analysis. Obesity Reviews. 2023;**24**(6):e13561

[78] Hsu LKG. Can dieting cause an eating disorder? Psychological Medicine. 1997;**27**(3):509-513

[79] Martin-Biggers J, Quick V, Spaccarotella K, Byrd-Bredbenner C. An exploratory study examining obesity risk in non-obese mothers of young children using a socioecological approach. Nutrients. 2018;**10**(6):781

[80] Jebeile H et al. Identifying factors which influence eating disorder risk during behavioral weight management: A consensus study. Nutrients. 2023;**15**(5):1-17

[81] Eckel RH et al. Obesity and type 2 diabetes: What can be unified and what needs to be individualized? The Journal of Clinical Endocrinology and Metabolism. 2011;**96**(6):1654-1663

[82] Bell DSH. Type 2 diabetes mellitus: What is the optimal treatment regimen? The American Journal of Medicine. 2004;**116**(5, Suppl. 1):23-29

[83] Knowler WC, Barrett-Connor E, Fowler SE, Hamman RF, Lachin JM, Walker EA, et al. Reduction in the incidence of type 2 diabetes with lifestyle intervention or metformin.

The New England Journal of Medicine. 2002;**346**(6):393-403

[84] Diabetes Prevention Program Research Group. 10-year follow-up of diabetes incidence and weight loss in the diabetes prevention program outcomes study. Lancet. 2009;**374**(9702):1677-1686

[85] Uusitupa M et al. The Finnish diabetes prevention study. The British Journal of Nutrition. 2000;**83**(S1): S137-S142

[86] Gong Q et al. Morbidity and mortality after lifestyle intervention for people with impaired glucose tolerance: 30-year results of the Da Qing Diabetes Prevention Outcome Study. The Lancet Diabetes and Endocrinology. 2019;**7**(6):452-461

[87] Dutton GR, Lewis CE. The look AHEAD trial: Implications for lifestyle intervention in type 2 diabetes mellitus. Progress in Cardiovascular Diseases. 2015;**58**(1):69-75

[88] Lauren L et al. Variability of body weight and health outcomes in the Framingham population. The New England Journal of Medicine. 1991;**324**(26):1839-1844

[89] Rubino F et al. Joint international consensus statement for ending stigma of obesity. Nature Medicine. 2020;**26**(4):485-497

[90] Gaesser GA, Angadi SS. Obesity treatment: Weight loss versus increasing fitness and physical activity for reducing health risks. iScience. 2021;**24**(10):102995

[91] Ross R, Bradshaw AJ. The future of obesity reduction: Beyond weight loss. Nature Reviews. Endocrinology. 2009;**5**(6):319-325

[92] Samuel K et al. Absence of an effect of liposuction on insulin action and risk factors for coronary heart disease. The New England Journal of Medicine. 2025;**350**(25):2549-2557

[93] Gil S et al. Constraints of weight loss as a marker of bariatric surgery success: An exploratory study. Frontiers in Physiology. 2021;**12**:640191

[94] Sonneville KR, Austin B. Does addressing obesity create risk for eating disorders? In: Brownell KD, Walsh BT, editors. Eating Disorders and Obesity: A Comprehensive Handbook. 3rd ed. New York: Routledge; 2017. pp. 152-162

[95] O'Hara L, Gregg J. The war on obesity: A social determinant of health. Health Promotion Journal of Australia. 2006;**17**(3):260-263

[96] O'Hara L, Taylor J. What's wrong with the 'war on obesity?' A narrative review of the weight-centered health paradigm and development of the 3C framework to build critical competency for a paradigm shift. SAGE Open. 2018;**8**(2):2158244018772888

[97] Mauldin K, May M, Clifford D. The consequences of a weight-centric approach to healthcare: A case for a paradigm shift in how clinicians address body weight. Nutrition in Clinical Practice. 2022;**37**(6):1291-1306

[98] Hunger JM, Smith JP, Tomiyama AJ. An evidence-based rationale for adopting weight-inclusive health policy. Social Issues and Policy Review. 2020;**14**(1):73-107

[99] Hoare JK, Lister NB, Garnett SP, Baur LA, Jebeile H. Weight-neutral interventions in young people with high body mass index: A systematic review. Nutrition and Dietetics. 2023;**80**(1):8-20

[100] Bacon L, Aphramor L. Weight science: Evaluating the evidence for a paradigm shift. Nutrition Journal. 2011;**10**(1):9

[101] Clifford D, Ozier A, Bundros J, Moore J, Kreiser A, Morris MN. Impact of non-diet approaches on attitudes, behaviors, and health outcomes: A systematic review. Journal of Nutrition Education and Behavior. 2015;**47**(2):143-155.e1

[102] Ulian MD et al. Effects of health at every size® interventions on health-related outcomes of people with overweight and obesity: A systematic review. Obesity Reviews. 2018;**19**(12):1659-1666

[103] Ralph AF et al. Management of eating disorders for people with higher weight: Clinical practice guideline. Journal of Eating Disorders. 2022;**10**(1):121

[104] Kantilafti M, Chrysostomou S, Yannakoulia M, Giannakou K. The association between binge eating disorder and weight management in overweight and obese adults: A systematic literature review. Nutrition and Health. 2021;**28**(2):189-197

[105] Fischer M, Oberänder N, Weimann A. Four main barriers to weight loss maintenance? A quantitative analysis of difficulties experienced by obese patients after successful weight reduction. European Journal of Clinical Nutrition. 2020;**74**(8):1192-1200

[106] Yanovski SZ. Binge eating disorder and obesity in 2003: Could treating an eating disorder have a positive effect on the obesity epidemic? The International Journal of Eating Disorders. 2003;**34**(S1):S117-S120

[107] da Luz FQ, Hay P, Touyz S, Sainsbury A. Obesity with comorbid eating disorders: Associated health risks and treatment approaches. Nutrients. 2018;**10**(7):1-9

[108] Lebow J, Sim LA, Accurso EC. Is there clinical consensus in defining weight restoration for adolescents with anorexia nervosa? Eating Disorders. 2018;**26**(3):270-277

[109] Livhits M et al. Preoperative predictors of weight loss following bariatric surgery: Systematic review. Obesity Surgery. 2012;**22**(1):70-89

[110] Malik S, Mitchell JE, Engel S, Crosby R, Wonderlich S. Psychopathology in bariatric surgery candidates: A review of studies using structured diagnostic interviews. Comprehensive Psychiatry. 2014;**55**(2):248-259

[111] Mitchell JE et al. Psychopathology before surgery in the longitudinal assessment of bariatric surgery-3 (LABS-3) psychosocial study. Surgery for Obesity and Related Diseases. 2012;**8**(5):533-541

[112] Kops NL, Vivan MA, Fülber ER, Fleuri M, Fagundes J, Friedman R. Preoperative binge eating and weight loss after bariatric surgery: A systematic review and meta-analysis. Obesity Surgery. 2021;**31**(3):1239-1248

[113] Smith KE et al. Loss of control eating and binge eating in the 7 years following bariatric surgery. Obesity Surgery. 2019;**29**(6):1773-1780

[114] Mitchell JE et al. Postoperative behavioral variables and weight change 3 years after bariatric surgery. JAMA Surgery. 2016;**151**(8):752-757

[115] Meany G, Conceição E, Mitchell JE. Binge eating, binge eating disorder and loss of control eating: Effects on weight outcomes after bariatric surgery.

European Eating Disorders Review. 2014;**22**(2):87-91

[116] Chao AM et al. Binge-eating disorder and the outcome of bariatric surgery in a prospective, observational study: Two-year results. Obesity. 2016;**24**(11):2327-2333

[117] Pinto-Bastos A, de Lourdes M, Brandão I, Machado PPP, Conceição EM. Weight loss trajectories and psychobehavioral predictors of outcome of primary and reoperative bariatric surgery: A 2-year longitudinal study. Surgery for Obesity and Related Diseases. 2019;**15**(7):1104-1112

[118] Sarwer DB, Heinberg LJ. A review of the psychosocial aspects of clinically severe obesity and bariatric surgery. The American Psychologist. 2020;**75**(2):252-264

[119] Tess BH, Maximiano-Ferreira L, Pajecki D, Wang Y-P. Bariatric surgery and binge eating disorder: Should surgeons care about it? A literature review of prevalence and assessment tools. Arquivos de Gastroenterologia. 2019;**56**(1):55-60

[120] Sarwer DB et al. 4-year changes in sex hormones, sexual functioning, and psychosocial status in women who underwent bariatric surgery. Obesity Surgery. 2018;**28**(4):892-899

[121] McElroy SL, Guerdjikova AI, Mori N, Munoz MR, Keck PE. Overview of the treatment of binge eating disorder. CNS Spectrums. 2015;**20**(6):546-556

[122] Bradley LE, Forman EM, Kerrigan SG, Butryn ML, Herbert JD, Sarwer DB. A pilot study of an acceptance-based behavioral intervention for weight regain after bariatric surgery. Obesity Surgery. 2016;**26**(10):2433-2441

[123] Bradley LE, Thomas JG, Hood MM, Corsica JA, Kelly MC, Sarwer DB. Remote assessments and behavioral interventions in post-bariatric surgery patients. Surgery for Obesity and Related Diseases. 2018;**14**(10):1632-1644

[124] Hebebrand J, Antel J, Conceição E, Matthews A, Hinney A, Peters T. What amount of weight loss can entail anorexia nervosa or atypical anorexia nervosa after bariatric surgery? The International Journal of Eating Disorders. 2024;**57**(12): 2461-2468

[125] Taba JV et al. The development of feeding and eating disorders after bariatric surgery: A systematic review and Meta-analysis. Nutrients. 2021;**13**(7):2396

[126] Marino JM et al. The emergence of eating pathology after bariatric surgery: A rare outcome with important clinical implications. The International Journal of Eating Disorders. 2012;**45**(2):179-184

[127] Conceição E, Hilbert A. Atypical anorexia nervosa after bariatric surgery and the DSM-5 diagnostic criteria: Commentary on Walsh et al. (2023). The International Journal of Eating Disorders. 2023;**56**(4):831-834

[128] Brambilla F, Samek L, Company M, Lovo F, Cioni L, Mellado C. Multivariate therapeutic approach to binge-eating disorder: Combined nutritional, psychological and pharmacological treatment. International Clinical Psychopharmacology. 2009;**24**(6):312-317

[129] Devlin MJ et al. Cognitive behavioral therapy and fluoxetine as adjuncts to group behavioral therapy for binge eating disorder. Obesity Research. 2005;**13**(6):1077-1088

[130] Masheb RM, Grilo CM, Rolls BJ. A randomized controlled trial for obesity and binge eating disorder: Low-energy-density dietary counseling

and cognitive-behavioral therapy. Behaviour Research and Therapy. 2011;**49**(12):821-829

[131] Grilo CM, Masheb RM, Wilson GT, Gueorguieva R, White MA. Cognitive–behavioral therapy, behavioral weight loss, and sequential treatment for obese patients with binge-eating disorder: A randomized controlled trial. Journal of Consulting and Clinical Psychology. 2011;**79**(5):675-685

[132] Peat CM et al. Comparative effectiveness of treatments for binge-eating disorder: Systematic review and network meta-analysis. European Eating Disorders Review. 2017;**25**(5):317-328

[133] Paranjothy SM, Wade TD. A meta-analysis of disordered eating and its association with self-criticism and self-compassion. The International Journal of Eating Disorders. 2024;**57**(3):473-536

[134] Dalle Grave R. GLP-1RAs in People With Higher Weight and Eating Disorders [Online]. 2024. Available from: https://www.psychologytoday.com/intl/blog/eating-disorders-the-facts/202412/glp-1ras-in-people-with-higher-weight-and-eating-disorders [Accessed: January 5, 2025]

[135] Bartel S, McElroy SL, Levangie D, Keshen A. Use of glucagon-like peptide-1 receptor agonists in eating disorder populations. The International Journal of Eating Disorders. 2024;**57**(2):286-293

[136] Balantekin KN, Kretz MJ, Mietlicki-Baase EG. The emerging role of glucagon-like peptide 1 in binge eating. The Journal of Endocrinology. 2024;**262**(1):e230405

[137] Ralph A et al. Management of Eating Disorders for People with Higher Weight: Clinical Practice Guideline. Australia: National Eating Disorders Collaboration (NEDC); 2022